KING ARTHUR

Other books in the Heroes and Villains series include:

Heroes and Villains

KING ARTHUR

Don Nardo

LUCENT
BOOKS ®

THOMSON
─────★─────™
GALE

San Diego • Detroit • New York • San Francisco • Cleveland • New Haven, Conn. • Waterville, Maine • London • Munich

THOMSON

GALE

™

© 2003 by Lucent Books. Lucent Books is an imprint of The Gale Group, Inc.,
a division of Thomson Learning, Inc.

Lucent Books® and Thomson Learning™ are trademarks used herein under license.

For more information, contact
Lucent Books
27500 Drake Rd.
Farmington Hills, MI 48331-3535
Or you can visit our Internet site at http://www.gale.com

LIBRARY OF CONGRESS CATALOGING-IN-PUBLICATION DATA

Nardo, Don, 1947–
    King Arthur / by Don Nardo.
        p. cm. — (Heroes and villains series)
Summary: Surveys the known history of King Arthur, the legends and lore sur-
rounding him, his treatment in literature, and the possible historical background
of his associates and stories.
Includes bibliographical references and index.
    ISBN 1-56006-948-1 (alk. paper)
    1. Arthur, King—Juvenile literature. 2. Britons—Kings and rulers—Juvenile
literature. 3. Great Britain—History—To 1066—Juvenile literature. 4. Great
Britain—Antiquities, Celtic—Juvenile literature. 5. Arthurian romances—History
and criticism—Juvenile literature. [1. Arthur, King. 2. Arthur, King—Legends.
3. Kings, queens, rulers, etc. 4. Great Britain—History—To 1066. 5. Knights and
knighthood—Folklore. 6. Folklore—England.] I. Title. II. Series.
    DA152.5.A7 N37 2003
    942.01'4—dc21
                                                                    2001008668

Printed in the United States of America

Contents

Good and evil are an ever-present feature of human history. Their presence is reflected through the ages in tales of great heroism and extraordinary villainy. Such tales provide insight into human nature, whether they involve two people or two thousand, for the essence of heroism and villainy is found in deeds rather than in numbers. It is the deeds that pique our interest and lead us to wonder what prompts a man or woman to perform such acts.

Samuel Johnson, the eminent eighteenth-century English writer, once wrote, "The two great movers of the human mind are the desire for good, and fear of evil." The pairing of desire and fear, possibly two of the strongest human emotions, helps explain the intense fascination people have with all things good and evil—and by extension, heroic and villainous.

People are attracted to the person who reaches into a raging river to pull a child from what could have been a watery grave for both, and to the person who risks his or her own life to shepherd hundreds of desperate black slaves to safety on the Underground Railroad. We wonder what qualities these heroes possess that enable them to act against self-interest, and even their own survival. We also wonder if, under similar circumstances, we would behave as they do.

Evil, on the other hand, horrifies as well as intrigues us. Few people can look upon the drifter who mutilates and kills a neighbor or the dictator who presides over the torture and murder of thousands of his own citizens without feeling a sense of revulsion. And yet, as Joseph Conrad writes, we experience "the fascination of the abomination." How else to explain the overwhelming success of a book such as Truman Capote's *In Cold Blood*, which examines in horrifying detail a vicious and senseless murder that took place in the American heartland in the 1960s? The popularity of murder mysteries and Court TV are also evidence of the human fascination with villainy.

Most people recoil in the face of such evil. Yet most feel a deep-seated curiosity about the kind of person who could commit a terrible act. It is perhaps a reflection of our innermost fears that we wonder whether we could resist or stand up to such behavior in our presence or even if we ourselves possess the capacity to commit such terrible crimes.

The Lucent Books Heroes and Villains series capitalizes on our fascination with the perpetrators of both good and evil by introducing readers to some of history's most revered heroes and hated villains. These include heroes such as Frederick Douglass, who knew firsthand the humiliation of slavery and, at great risk to himself, publicly fought to abolish the institution of slavery in America. It also includes villains such as Adolf Hitler, who is remembered both for the devastation of Europe and for the murder of 6 million Jews and thousands of Gypsies, Slavs, and others whom Hitler deemed unworthy of life.

Each book in the Heroes and Villains series examines the life story of a hero or villain from history. Generous use of primary and secondary source quotations gives readers eyewitness views of the life and times of each individual as well as enlivens the narrative. Notes and annotated bibliographies provide stepping-stones to further research.

Arthur's Place in Western Culture

King Arthur is one of the most recognizable characters in the annals of Western civilization. He is also one of the most revered, respected, and beloved of its heroes because he is remembered as a man of uncommon virtue, valor, and honor. A handful of other Western personages are remembered for similar qualities, among them Joan of Arc, Sir Thomas More, George Washington, Abraham Lincoln, Mohandas Gandhi, and Martin Luther King. The major difference between these cultural heroes and King Arthur is that they were real historical figures whose lives and deeds can be documented, whereas he remains a mythical figure. Arthur may or may not have been real. And even if he *was* a real person, it is virtually certain that his splendid court at Camelot and the wondrous deeds attributed to him and his knights are mostly exaggerations and/or fabrications.

That is what makes Arthur's image so unique in Western culture. People of all ages and walks of life have viewed and continue to view him as a role model, a truly good person to emulate, *even if he never existed*. In a way, a mythical figure has come to have a tangible existence in society's collective consciousness and in the hearts and minds of individuals. More accurately, more than one Arthur exists, since different people learn about him and come to view his image in different ways. As Marymount University scholar Christopher Snyder puts it, there was

a folkloric or mythological Arthur who came to be mistaken for a living person. There was a literary Arthur, indeed several, and an Arthur portrayed in almost every other artistic medium. There was, and is, a "figure" of Arthur made up of all these elements, who has made a very real impact on history because he has made a very deep impression in the hearts of so many men and women, for more than a thousand years.[1]

The Arthurian Mythos

Indeed, Arthur's varied mythology, often collectively called the Arthurian legends, has developed over the course of perhaps fourteen centuries. And through all these ages, he has been a sort of shape-shifter, "subtly and slowly changing his form to suit the needs of each new age,"[2] in the words of noted Arthurian scholar Richard Barber. For a long time the main vehicle for the evolving Arthur was literature, as various poems and stories borrowed from or built and expanded on those that came before. Especially in late medieval France and England, popular romances (colorful tales of love, heroism, and chivalry) made

Among the thousands of artistic renditions in the Arthurian mythos is this fourteenth-century illustration from a French manuscript *The Romance of King Arthur.*

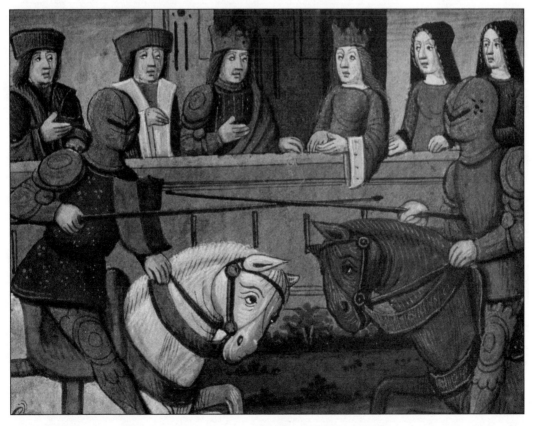

Arthur and Camelot loom large in the public mind. Entirely new characters and subplots were created in these years. Arthur's friend and trusted knight Lancelot, for example, seems to have been created by the French poets; he does not appear in the traditional medieval Welsh tales that contain the earliest versions of Arthur's legends.

The sum total of all these characters and stories is much too complex and diverse to be called a mere myth. A more descriptive term would be the Arthurian "mythos"—that is, all of the divergent Arthurian characters, poems, stories, artistic renditions, and scholarly and popular theories about Arthur's identity that have been collected over the years. This collection is not set in stone; to the contrary, it continues to grow and expand at an ever-increasing rate, as Arthur's heroic image implants itself deeper and deeper into the Western psyche. "In recent years Arthurian myth-making has gone mad," Arthurian scholar Graham Phillips points out.

One of many artistic representations of Arthur's famous round table, where each of his many knights occupied a seat of equal prominence.

Some of the more extreme notions are mind-boggling, from Arthur being an extraterrestrial to his being the king of Atlantis. One recent theory, which actually gained a degree of acceptance, claimed that he was the first European to discover America. Obsessives have spent a fortune trying to track him down; indeed whole societies have been formed for this express purpose. Some even claim to have discovered his remains, while others have resorted to staging elaborate hoaxes as "proof." . . . There are guide books, lecture tours, coach trips, magazines, and video tapes available for the enthusiast, even travel companies offering Arthurian Holidays. King Arthur is arguably the most popular character in British history.[3]

"Camelot Speaks to Us"

Arthur is hardly less popular in the United States, where poems, novels, scholarly books, music, Broadway shows, movies, college courses, toys, video games, and Internet websites devoted to Arthur and the chivalrous world of Camelot abound. This shows that the Arthurian legends are not dead myths buried away with prior generations and revived from time to time as scholarly curiosities. "Camelot still speaks to us," Snyder writes.

> As [the famous British leader] Winston Churchill asserted, [Arthur and his heroic image are] a lasting and important part of our Western cultural inheritance, like the stories of Homer and the Bible, to be drawn upon whenever we want to express our societal hopes and fears. "It is all true," wrote Churchill of the Arthurian legends, "or it ought to be."[4]

Thus, King Arthur, in the guise of a Western leader struggling to find the path of truth and morality, is as much a hero today as in any past age. In an imperfect world, he has come to personify our inner longings for the kind of society he is said to have ruled "for one brief shining moment"[5] in the mists of history—one in which might does not *make* right but is used *for* right.

Chapter One

ARTHUR IN HISTORY, LEGEND, AND LITERATURE

Who was King Arthur? Was he a real person who ruled part or all of early Britain and accomplished deeds remembered through the ages? Or was he just an imaginary figure conjured up by medieval chroniclers, minstrels, and poets? These questions have haunted scholars, as well as untold numbers of ordinary people, for more than a thousand years. And over the centuries, hundreds of writers have attempted to identify Arthur, to put a historical face on one of the great folk heroes of Western culture.

The search for Arthur has been and continues to be daunting. This is partly because the place and age in which he lived (if he was indeed a real person)—Britain in the fifth and sixth centuries—are very ancient and wrapped in mystery. Also, all of the historical and literary sources in which Arthur appears were composed centuries after the fact. The earliest ones—those closest to his time—mention him only briefly; and the longer, more detailed, more famous versions of his story are products of late medieval times, at least eight or nine hundred years removed from their principal subject. For these reasons, investigators must work backward. They typically begin by considering the later, full-blown tales about Arthur and then search the older sources for clues to people, places, and events mentioned in these tales.

The full-blown Arthurian stories vary considerably in their focus and details. But the basic elements, common to most, picture Arthur as a Christian monarch who ruled much or all of the British countryside from a castle called Camelot. His most intimate adviser, who in some versions of the story tutors him and helps him gain the throne, is Merlin, an old man with prophetic or magical powers.

Once in power, Arthur gathers around him the Knights of the Round Table. Each knight, known for his superior valor and fighting ability, swears to support the king and uphold a strict code of chivalry. A number of versions have Arthur and his followers fight various invaders (the most menacing being the Saxons, who are defeated at Mount Badon). Some of the knights also go on quests to find the Holy Grail, the cup supposedly used by Jesus Christ at the Last Supper; but only Sir Galahad is pure enough of heart to be allowed to find and hold the Grail. Another of Arthur's knights, Sir Lancelot, has a love affair with the king's wife, Guinevere; this sin, coupled with the attempt of Arthur's nephew (or son) Mordred to usurp the throne, brings about the collapse of the Round Table. In a great battle fought at Camlann, Mordred is slain and Arthur is mortally wounded; some followers carry the fallen king to the mysterious Isle of Avalon, where he will be healed and there wait until called on in some future age to return and rule Britain once again.

Witnesses to Early Medieval Britain

Arthurian scholars would naturally prefer to find references to some of these characters and events in documents from fifth- and sixth-century Britain. Only two marginally substantial sources written by Britons have survived from that period. One is a short autobiography of Saint Patrick, a British Christian who

This magnificent statue of Arthur rests in the Royal Chapel at Innsbruck, Austria.

An old engraving depicts Lancelot and Guinevere, whose love affair entered the Arthurian legends several centuries after the real Arthur supposedly existed.

did missionary work in Ireland; the other is a longer letterlike narrative, *On the Ruin of Britain,* by a British clergyman named Gildas. Neither Patrick nor Gildas mentions Arthur, Camelot, the Round Table, Guinevere, or Mordred. One would think that if these people and things did exist at the time, the two writers would have alluded to them somehow. One possibility is that the historical Arthur, if any, came to power shortly *after* Patrick and Gildas wrote their tracts.

It is interesting to note that Gildas does mention the battle fought at Mount Badon, which modern scholars view as a real event that occurred about A.D. 500. Gildas tells how, after the Romans lost control of Britain, the Saxons and other "barbarian" peoples invaded the country. This squares with reliable historical evidence showing that the Romans abandoned their once-prosperous province of Britannia in A.D. 410, after which the island steadily fell under the sway of Saxons, Angles, Jutes, and other Germanic invaders from Europe. The local Britons, made up of a mixture of Celts (the original inhabitants of the island) and Romans who had intermarried with the natives, were eventually conquered and absorbed into an Anglo-Saxon melting pot.

Returning to Gildas's account, for years the Saxons and other invaders caused widespread lawlessness, pillage, and misery. Then a war leader named Ambrosius Aurelianus (perhaps the grandson of a former Roman army commander) rallied the Britons. "Under him," Gildas says, our people regained their strength, and challenged the victors to battle. . . . From then on victory went now to our countrymen, now to their enemies. . . . This lasted right up till the year of the siege of Badon Hill, pretty well the last defeat of the villains, and certainly not the least. That was the year of my birth; as I know, one month of the forty-fourth year since then has already elapsed.[6]

Was Ambrosius Aurelianus the historical Arthur? Possibly. But if so, with the exception of the victory at Mount Badon, he did not accomplish any of the heroic and romantic deeds described in the Arthurian stories. Nor, for that matter,

did any of his contemporaries. After all, Gildas himself would have witnessed the rise of a kingdom as strong, peaceful, prosperous, just, and chivalrous as Camelot; yet of the Britain of his day, he writes: "The cities of our land are not populated even now as they once were; right to the present they are deserted, in ruins and unkempt. . . . All the controls of truth and justice have been shaken and overthrown, leaving no trace."[7]

Was Arthur a Local Warlord?
The first actual historical references to Arthur appear in the anonymous *Welsh Annals (Annales Cambriae)* and the *History of the Britons (Historia Brittonum)*. Both works are difficult to date, but the

A Dragon Threatens Arthur's Lands

One of the early literary references to Arthur is in an anonymous Welsh document known as The Life of St. Carannog *(quoted here from Richard White's* King Arthur in Legend and History*), written about 1100. The king requests the saint's assistance in fighting a dragon. (Arthur's follower Cato is likely an early version of his knight Sir Kay.)*

St. Carannog returned to his own homeland of Cardigan. . . . At that time Cato and Arthur were ruling in this region . . . and as Arthur was traveling around he came across an enormous, terrible, and most powerful dragon, which had devastated a twelfth of the fields. . . . Then Carannog came and greeted Arthur [who asked the holy man to subdue the dragon]. . . . Behold the dragon came with a great noise . . . and bowed its head before God's servant . . . with a humble heart and downcast eyes. The saint placed his robe around its neck and led it like a lamb; it did not raise up its wings or its claws. . . . [Carannog] led it through the fortress gate and dismissed it, ordering it to injure nobody and to return no more, and it departed. . . . Then King Arthur said, "Carannog should be given a twelfth part of the fields."

consensus of scholars is that they were written in the eighth or ninth century. The *Annals* consists of lists of dates, each followed by a short entry about an important event. Following are the two that mention Arthur:

> [A.D. 518, the year of] the Battle of [Mount] Badon, in which Arthur bore the cross of our Lord Jesus Christ on his shoulders for three days and three nights, and the Britons were the victors.

> [A.D. 539, the year of the] Battle of Camlann, in which Arthur and Medraut perished; and there was plague in Britain and Ireland.[8]

Gildas mentions only one Arthurian element—the battle at Mount Badon; whereas the *Annals* lists four—Mount Badon, Arthur, the Battle of Camlann, and Medraut, an early spelling of Mordred. Although the entry about Camlann says that Arthur and Mordred both died there, it does not say whether

The legendary Arthur and his trusty knights come to life in this evocative illustration by noted French painter Gustave Dore.

they fought each other or on the same side; nor is Mordred identified as Arthur's nephew.

The *History of the Britons* tells how a British king named Vortigern was betrayed by a Saxon mercenary, after which the Saxons tried to overrun the country. Arthur is described not as a king but a war leader who aided the British kings by defeating the Saxons in twelve battles. "The twelfth battle was on Mount Badon," the text reads, "in which nine hundred and sixty men fell in one day from one charge by Arthur, and no one overthrew them except himself alone."[9]

The most significant aspect of this narrative is that it portrays Arthur as a warlord supporting a group of British kings. This has a ring of truth to it for two reasons. First, it does stand to reason that Roman Britannia would have broken up into several small Romano-Celtic kingdoms after its abandonment by Rome's central authority in the early fifth century. Second, the text uses the Latin title *dux bellorum* to describe Arthur. A *dux*, the origin of the title duke, was a late Roman military leader, so that *dux bellorum* translates as "war duke" or "war commander." This clue led a number of modern scholars, including historian R.G. Collingwood, to view Arthur, like Ambrosius Aurelianus, as one of a group of British warlords who still maintained some of the old Roman military ranks and traditions.

Archaeologist Leslie Alcock, who excavated a post-Roman hill fort at South Cadbury (in southern England) in the 1960s, also suggests that Arthur might have been a local warlord. Many people have come to associate Cadbury with Camelot. Although Alcock himself does not specifically endorse this idea, he points out that Cadbury was an unusually strong and strategically important military installation in the period in question. "It seems unlikely that this eighteen-acre fort," Alcock writes,

> was intended as a prince's defended homestead. . . . It seems most likely to have served as the base for an army that was large by the standards of the time. This might have been recruited widely . . . or might have combined the war-bands of several kingdoms for the defense of southern and western Britain against Saxons on the south coast and in the Thames [River] valley. Within our present framework of knowledge, it seems plain enough that Cadbury-Camelot played some special part in the warfare of southern Britain in the late fifth and sixth centuries.[10]

Other Candidates for Arthur and Camelot

Although this circumstantial evidence supports the notion that the real Arthur, if such a person actually existed, was a successful British warlord based in southern England, many other theories have been proposed over the years. Some

The sprawling ruins at Tintagel, on England's southwestern coast, are among several places thought to be the site of Arthur's Camelot.

writers have maintained that Arthur was a full-fledged king, just as the legends claim. Usually, though, they picture him as only one of several local monarchs scattered across an England badly fragmented by the political and military upheavals of the fifth century.

One of the more intriguing of these hypotheses, championed by noted Arthurian scholar Geoffrey Ashe in the 1980s, is that the legendary Arthur was based on a firmly documented British king. In the late 460s, Anthemius, one of the last Western Roman emperors, faced the problem of the tribal Visigoths seizing control of Gaul, what is now France. Though Britain was no longer part of the Roman Empire by

this time, Anthemius appealed to a British king named Riothamus for aid in stopping the Visigoths. Riothamus agreed and led his army into Gaul, but his expedition ended in failure after he was betrayed by one of his own lieutenants. Ashe points out that in some later accounts Arthur fights enemies in France. The *Legend of St. Goeznovius*, dating from a little after A.D. 1000, for example, states that Arthur won "many splendid victories . . . in parts of Britain and Gaul."[11] (This document also implies that Arthur somehow transcended death after his worldly work was finished; later Arthurian stories and legends carry the idea further, claiming Arthur is waiting somewhere to be recalled.)

As for the location of Arthur's kingdom, various towns and ruined sites have been suggested as Camelot. Besides South Cadbury, southern England has Tintagel (on the southwestern coast). Wales also has several proposed Arthurian sites, among them Caerleon, which has extensive Roman ruins and bears the nickname "Arthur's Table." By contrast, a number of writers, recently including noted scholar Norma Goodrich, place the Arthurian realm farther north, along the border of England and Scotland.

Geoffrey of Monmouth's Arthur

The Arthur pictured as a warlord in the *History of the Britons* and a king in the *Legend of St. Goeznovius* may or may not have been a real person. What is significant is that in these documents he is able to defeat 960 men in a single charge and to transcend earthly death; clearly, by the close of the first millennium, he had already begun to take on mythical heroic qualities. And other short Arthurian accounts that circulated through Britain in the century or so that followed added more fanciful details to the growing mystique.

The first major work to combine elements of these early works into a single, complete narrative of Arthur's life was English (or Welsh) chronicler Geoffrey of Monmouth's *History of the Kings of Britain (Historia Regum Britanniae),*

Another proposed site for Camelot, Arthur's Table, at Caerleon in Wales, consists of the partially buried remains of an ancient Roman amphitheater.

compiled about 1136. The full text attempts to trace all the British rulers from the age of the Trojan War to the seventh-century A.D. Welsh kings. The section on Arthur, making up a full third of the work, was the first Arthurian tract to make Arthur widely famous beyond Britain.

According to Geoffrey, Arthur was the son of a British king, Uther Pendragon, and the nephew of Uther's brother, Aurelius Ambrosius (whom Gildas called Ambrosius Aurelianus). After succeeding Uther on the throne, Arthur carried on the fight against the Saxons. His major victory came at Bath (which many scholars believe is the site of the legendary Mount Badon), north of South Cadbury. According to Geoffrey, Arthur

put on a leather jerkin worthy of so great a king. On his head he placed a golden helmet, with a crest carved in the shape of a dragon; and across his shoulders a circular shield . . . on which was painted a likeness of the Blessed Mary, Mother of God. . . . Arthur drew up his men . . . and then bravely attacked the Saxons. . . . All that day they resisted the Britons bravely, although the latter launched attack upon attack. Finally, towards

Arthur Slays a Giant

In this episode from Geoffrey of Monmouth's History of the Kings of Britain, *Arthur and two of his knights confront a fearsome giant who has been terrorizing a region of northern France.*

At that moment the inhuman monster was standing by his fire. His face was smeared with the clotted blood of a number of pigs at which he had been gnawing.... The moment he saw the newcomers [Arthur and the two knights] . . . he rushed to snatch up his club, which two young men would have found difficulty lifting off the ground. The king drew his sword from his scabbard . . . and rushed forward at full speed....The giant . . . took up his club and dealt the king such a mighty blow on his shield that . . . the reverberation of the impact deafened Arthur's ears completely. The king grew white-hot in the fierceness of his rage. He struck the giant on the forehead with his sword and . . . the blood ran down his face and into his eyes and prevented him from seeing.... Blinded as he was, he rushed forward all the more fiercely.... Moving like lightning, [Arthur] struck the giant repeatedly with his sword . . . giving him no respite until he had dealt him a lethal blow.... At this the evil creature gave one great shriek and toppled to the ground with a mighty crash.

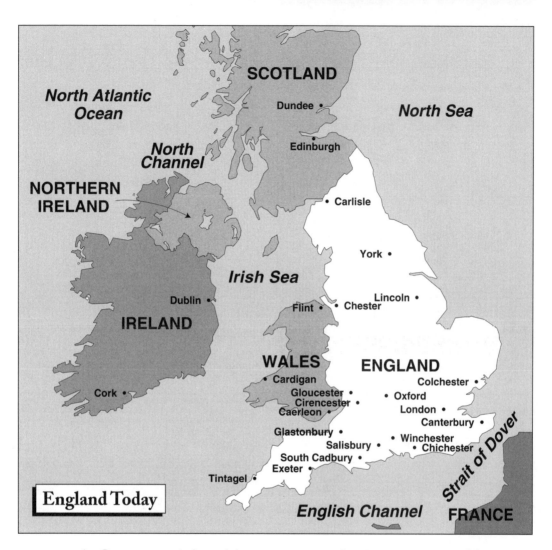

England Today

SCOTLAND

North Atlantic Ocean

North Sea

Dundee •

North Channel

Edinburgh •

NORTHERN IRELAND

• Carlisle

York •

Irish Sea

Dublin •

Lincoln •
Flint • • Chester

IRELAND

WALES   ENGLAND

Cardigan •   Colchester •
Cork •   Gloucester •   • Oxford
                Cirencester •   London •
                Caerleon •   Canterbury •
            Glastonbury •   • Winchester
                    Salisbury •   • Chichester
                South Cadbury •
        Tintagel • Exeter •

English Channel   FRANCE

Strait of Dover

sunset, the Saxons occupied a neighboring hill [Mount Badon?]. . . . When the next day dawned, Arthur climbed to the top of the peak with his army. . . . [They] reached the summit by a superlative effort and immediately engaged the enemy in hand-to-hand resistance. . . . The Saxons, who only a short time before used to attack like lightning in the most ferocious way imaginable, now ran away with fear in their hearts.[12]

Besides the Saxons, Geoffrey's Arthur defeats the Scots and some enemies in Gaul (as in the *Legend of St. Goeznovius*), as well as a man-eating giant. Geoffrey also portrays Arthur holding court in lavish surroundings, staging tournaments in which chivalrous knights joust,

21

This illustration of Sir Perceval and Sir Lancelot attacking Sir Galahad is from a fifteenth-century edition of the *Romance of Saint Graal*.

and marrying a young woman named Guinevere (probably based on Gwenhwyfar, the name of three different women wed by Arthur in the old Welsh tales). The queen is unfaithful to her husband, but not with Lancelot, who was introduced into the legends later; in Geoffrey's version, she plots with Mordred (here portrayed as Arthur's nephew) to usurp the throne. At Camlann, Arthur defeats and kills Mordred but is wounded and carried away to the Isle of Avalon.

The Arthurian Romances

Geoffrey's chronicle of Arthur, which contains many romantic elements drawn from legend and hearsay, served as the principal basis for many later and quite fanciful romances. The first of the numerous French, German, and English Arthurian romances were five composed by Frenchman Chrétien de Troyes in the 1170s and 1180s—*Eric and Enide; Cligès; Lancelot, or The Knight of the Cart; Yvain, or The Knight of the Lion;* and *Perceval, or The Story of the Grail.* Chrétien introduced Lancelot and his love affair with Guinevere, and he is also the first writer to mention the fabulous Grail and tell how some of Arthur's knights dedicated themselves to finding it. In addition, Chrétien's *Lancelot* contains the first known literary reference to Camelot and its stately and colorful court:

King Arthur, one Ascension Day . . . held a most magnificent court at Camelot with all the splendor appropriate to the day. . . . In the hall there were many nobles; and the queen was there too and with her, I believe, numerous beautiful courtly ladies conversing easily in French.[13]

More Arthurian romances appeared in the three centuries following Chrétien de Troyes. Among them were stories about the individual adventures of several

This is one of many medieval depictions of Perceval and the Holy Grail.

of Arthur's knights, including elaborations on their quests for the Grail. One of the most important of these is a long anonymous work, *The Quest of the Holy Grail*, dating to about 1225, which deals with the quests of Lancelot, Perceval, Gawain, Galahad, and others. This work was one of several in what has come to be called the Vulgate Cycle. The narratives go into a great deal of detail, almost all of it surely fanciful, about Arthur, Lancelot, Merlin, and other key Arthurian characters. Later English Arthurian romances include the anonymous *Of Arthur and of Merlin* (ca. 1270–1300), *Ywain and Gawain* (ca. 1350), *Sir Gawain and the Green Knight* (ca. 1385–1390), and *The Avowing of Arthur* (ca. 1425), as well as Henry Lovelich's *The Romance of Merlin* (ca. 1450).

An Arthur for the Ages

The culmination of the English Arthurian tradition, and of premodern Arthurian literature in general, is Sir Thomas Malory's *Le Morte d'Arthur* (*Death of Arthur*), published in 1485. This magnificent work—which draws on a number of earlier sources about Arthur, especially the Vulgate Cycle—covers Arthur's story in its entirety in powerful, often moving prose. "Within the ponderous elaborations of the Vulgate Cycle," writes Richard Barber,

there lay hidden a great epic drama, ranging through every human passion, joy, and grief. Malory drew out the noble tragedy of Arthur from the mass of adventures and marvels in which it had become entangled, and gave to it a new unity and clarity. He made its protagonists [main characters] real people . . . and gave to the climax a befitting majesty and grandeur which it had never before attained. . . . He ensured that the Arthurian tradition . . . did not become a mere literary curiosity . . . but would re-emerge to inspire new masterpieces.[14]

Indeed, ever since it appeared, Malory's telling of Arthur's story has been widely viewed as the definitive one, in a way an "Arthur for the ages," and as such the leading primary source for the legendary events of Arthur's life. Hundreds of complete and abridged editions have appeared (including many in the twentieth century), most of them handsomely illustrated. And *Le Morte d'Arthur* has served as the inspiration for numerous modern Arthurian works; probably the most famous of these are Alfred Tennyson's long poem *Idylls of the King* (completed in 1869), and T.H. White's marvelous novel, *The Once and Future King* (1958). The latter, in its turn, inspired the 1960 hit Broadway musical *Camelot* (starring Richard Burton and Julie Andrews), which in 1967 became a movie (starring Richard Harris and Vanessa Redgrave).

The *Quest's* Uncertain Author and Date

The anonymous medieval work titled The Quest of the Holy Grail, *part of the Vulgate Cycle, tells of the search by several of Arthur's knights for the Holy Grail, or Sangreal, said to be the cup used by Jesus Christ during the Last Supper. In the introduction to his translation of the work, P.M. Matarasso discusses its possible author and date.*

The penultimate [next to the last] sentence of the *Quest* states that its author is one Walter Map, who at King Henry's instigation translated into French the records of the adventures of Arthur's knights preserved in the library at Salisbury. This, the only information we are given about the author, is quite undoubtedly untrue. Walter Map, archdeacon of Oxford . . . and protégé of Henry II, could not have written the *Quest* because he died in 1209, while modern scholarship is unanimous in dating the composition . . . [to] somewhere between 1215 and 1230. Since it seems likely that the writing of the work was spread over some 15 years, it is reasonable to set an approximate date of 1225 for the *Quest*. The identity of the author remains, and doubtless will remain, unknown.

Richard Burton as Arthur and Julie Andrews as Guinevere in Lerner and Loewe's *Camelot,* which opened on Broadway in 1960.

The legendary story of Arthur's life told in the following pages is based principally on selected episodes from Malory's definitive version, including some of the classic dialogue Malory supplied. However, a few incidents and details from other classic Arthurian sources, both medieval and modern, are also included. Excluded are most of the separate knights' adventures, as this telling concentrates on the central hero—Arthur—whose character continues to personify the highest qualities of goodness, courage, and justice for each new generation.

Chapter Two

The Coming of Arthur

Long ago, in the days when Uther Pendragon ruled England, the country witnessed much unrest and danger. Various highborn lords, each with a castle and many loyal armed men, held sway over local regions and territories. Many of these lords were ambitious and wished to be king, so their allegiance to Uther was often halfhearted and the prospect of rebellion and civil war was always real. What is more, the half-savage Picts and Scots threatened the kingdom's northern borders; while the uncouth Saxons, hailing from the little-known lands of Germany and Gaul across the English Channel, posed no less a threat to England's eastern coasts. Frequent raids by these peoples, along with widespread poverty and a general lack of concern for one's neighbors, made the country a bleak and uncertain place in which to live.

Uther's Mysterious Visitor

This was the unfortunate situation that existed when Uther's wife, Igraine, bore him a son, who stood someday to inherit the throne. Though the king wanted to raise the child himself, he did not; instead, even before christening and naming the baby, he told two of his knights to carry it to the castle's rear gate. There, he ordered, they were to give the child to a man wearing a long dark robe.

As the knights bore the child away, the king thought back to an episode that had transpired about two years before. Uther had sent for Merlin, an aged, mysterious man with a reputation as a far-seeing prophet and powerful magician. After this unusual visitor had arrived at the castle, the king stared at him in fascination. "Merlin had a long white beard," as one storyteller described him,

and long white moustaches which hung down on either side of it. Close inspection showed that he was far from clean. It was not that he had dirty fingernails, or anything like that, but some large bird seemed to have been nesting in his hair. . . . The old man was streaked with droppings over his shoulders, among the stars and triangles [sewn into] his gown, and a large spider was slowly lowering itself from the tip of his hat.[15]

Uther requested that Merlin perform a very vital service for the kingdom, and the old man agreed on the condition that the king would grant him anything he asked for in return. The king swore an oath to do so. Once Merlin had completed the task, he returned to Uther to collect his reward for services rendered. The king would have a son in the near future, the magician revealed. And when the time came, Uther must allow Merlin to take the newborn prince away and

This old etching pictures Merlin with a long white beard and a magician's dark robe and hat. Supposedly, he could foresee future events.

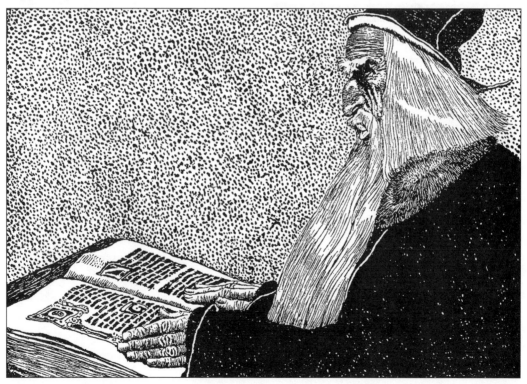

arrange for any upbringing that he, Merlin, saw fit. Uther was reluctant to consent to such a deal at first. But Merlin reminded him that he could see into the future and assured him the arrangement would eventually benefit the boy; moreover, Uther considered that he had sworn on his honor to grant Merlin anything he wanted; so the king finally agreed to the strange request.

Now that the boy had been born, only Uther knew that the man in a dark robe waiting at the rear gate was Merlin. The magician secretly took the child to the household of Sir Ector, a well-to-do knight known for his honesty and decency. Sir Ector and his wife called for a priest, who christened the boy. The couple then named the child Arthur, and they came to love him as much as their own son, Kay.

The Sword in the Stone

Only two years after Arthur had come to live in Sir Ector's home, Uther Pendragon fell sick and died. Because the king had left no apparent heir, the kingdom fell into a state of disarray, as numerous powerful nobles vied for the right to sit on the throne. Merlin wisely realized that the time was not yet right to reveal Arthur's true identity, as one or more of the royal claimants might kill the boy.

Merlin's Prophecies

In his History of the Kings of Britain, *Geoffrey of Monmouth lists numerous, mostly vague prophecies attributed to the mystical figure Merlin, among them:*

—Alas for the Red Dragon, for its end is near. Its cavernous dens shall be occupied by the White Dragon, which stands for the Saxons, whom you have invited over [the sea to England]. The Red Dragon represents the [native] people of Britain, who will be overrun by the White One, for Britain's mountains and valleys shall be leveled, and the streams in its valleys shall run with blood.

—A shower of blood shall fall and a dire famine shall afflict mankind.

—The Red One will grieve for what has happened, but after an immense effort it will regain its strength.

—Calamity will next pursue the White One and the buildings in its little garden will be torn down.

—Death will lay hands on the people and destroy all the nations. Those who are left alive will abandon their native soil and will sow their seeds in other men's fields.

Merlin paints an emblem on young Arthur's shield in this nineteenth-century illustration.

In the meantime, while the throne remained in doubt, Merlin tutored Arthur, teaching him how to ride horses, shoot a bow, swim, and also to talk to animals in their own tongues. Always, though, the magician was careful not to tell the boy that he was the former king's heir; Arthur continued quite naturally to assume he was Ector's son.

After several more years had passed, Merlin finally deemed that it was time for the kingdom to discover its rightful ruler. He went to the archbishop of Canterbury, the only figure in the country whom everyone venerated and trusted, and counseled him to gather together all the great lords in London at the upcoming Christmas celebration. There,

at St. Paul's Cathedral, a miracle would occur that would reveal the identity of the rightful king.

Sure enough, after the great congregation of lords and knights had prayed in the cathedral, someone noticed something strange in the church courtyard. It was, in Thomas Malory's words,

a great stone four-feet-square, like to a marble stone, and in the midst thereof was an anvil of steel, a foot of height, and therein stuck a fair sword . . . and letters of gold were written about the sword that said thus: "Whoso pulleth out this sword out of this stone and anvil is rightly King of all England."[16]

29

Pouring into the courtyard, each of the mighty men tried his hand at pulling the sword from the stone; but none could budge the weapon so much as a single inch, leaving everyone both exhausted and exasperated. "He is not yet here," said the archbishop, "that shall have the power to remove the sword, but doubt not that God will make him to be known."[17]

The Tournament

The fulfillment of the archbishop's prediction occurred in the following manner. He reasoned that the identity of the new king might be revealed by staging a tournament in which the greatest barons and knights in the country would joust with one another. The winner of these contests would be England's greatest warrior and worthy of ascending the throne. At the appointed time—New Year's Day—therefore, the lords and knights assembled on London's jousting field.

Among these notables were Sir Ector, whose estate was the largest in the region, and his son Sir Kay, now a strapping young man in his late teens. Arthur, who was a bit younger than Kay, came along to help his brother with his weapons, as well as to enjoy the spectacle. Indeed, like other young men who aspired to become knights, Arthur had been eagerly awaiting the tournament. He marveled at the sport and art of jousting and knew well that it took a great deal of strength, skill, and practice, for he himself was already attempting to master it. When two knights jousted, they used their right hands to hold their lances and guided their horses so that each man kept the handle of the lance on the opposite side of the body from the charging enemy. A knight held his shield on his left arm, so that he and the other jouster passed by each other shield to shield. There were many other factors to consider, among them how to hold one's lance, the size of the lance, where to aim it, and the best wood and methods to use in manufacturing it.

Miracle in the Churchyard

As Arthur pondered these technical aspects of weapons and fighting, his brother Kay approached with a worried look on his face. The older youth said that his sword was missing and guessed that he must have left it at home. Without a sword, Kay would not be allowed to compete in the contests, so Arthur immediately volunteered to ride home and fetch the weapon. Wasting no time, the young man leapt on his horse and raced back to Sir Ector's castle. Unfortunately, the sword was nowhere to be found.

Distraught at the thought that his brother might be excluded from the tournament, Arthur wracked his brain trying to think of where he might find another sword. Then it occurred to him that he had often seen a very fine-looking sword projecting from a stone in St. Paul's churchyard. "I will ride to the churchyard and take the sword," he shouted as he mounted his steed, "for my brother Sir Kay shall not be without a sword this day!"[18]

Reaching St. Paul's, Arthur went to the churchyard, which was deserted. He climbed up onto the stone, grasped the sword's handle, and pulled. The weapon came out easily, which did not surprise him, for no one had bothered to tell him about the difficulty others had encountered in removing the weapon. Rushing to the jousting field, Arthur found Kay and handed him the sword. The older youth saw that it was not his own and asked his brother where he had come by

Young Arthur draws the sword from the stone and proves himself to be the rightful king.

such a magnificent weapon. On hearing that this was the sword from the stone in St. Paul's churchyard, Kay told his father; and the three immediately set out for the cathedral.

When Sir Ector saw that the sword was missing from the stone, he declared in an awed tone of voice, "Now, Arthur, I understand that you must be king of this land."

"Why me?" Arthur asked.

"Sir," said Ector, "because there is no man who can draw out this sword who shall not rightwise be king of this land. Now let me see whether you can put the sword there as it was and pull it out again."

"That is no great feat," said Arthur; and so he put it in the stone.

This fourteenth-century painting depicts Arthur sitting on his throne.

Therewith, Sir Ector tried to pull out the sword and failed. "Now you try," said Sir Ector to Sir Kay, who pulled at the sword with all his might, but it would not be drawn.[19]

Now it was Arthur's turn. As his father and brother watched in breathless anticipation, he grasped the weapon and once more easily removed it from the stone. At that, Ector and Kay made the sign of the cross and knelt down before the astonished boy. He was the king, they said, and they were ready to serve him.

Soon afterward Sir Ector described the miracle in the churchyard to the archbishop, who called on all the lords and knights, as well as many common people, to come and witness the truth. Once more Arthur replaced the sword. All the nobles took their turns trying to pull it from the stone, and to no one's surprise, all failed as they had before. Then they watched Arthur remove it—the third time he had done so—and everyone stared in utter amazement that a mere boy had accomplished this feat. "We will have Arthur as our king!" they all cried at once, "for we all see that it is God's will that he shall be our king, and whoever opposes it we will slay!"[20] A few weeks later, the archbishop crowned Arthur king in a splendid coronation ceremony, and all the nobles in the land swore him their allegiance.

Igraine

In the year that followed Arthur's coronation, he devoted himself to consolidating his realm. There were a few lords living in the far north who had not seen him pull the sword from the stone and who refused to follow him. Taking five hundred of his best knights, the young king rode northward and challenged these nobles. It was not long before they saw that, despite his tender years, he was a strong ruler and heroic fighter; and they yielded to his kingly authority. Then Arthur took his army into Wales, where several local kings held sway over tiny kingdoms. These kings viewed him as a young upstart and besieged him and his knights in a fortress; but Arthur and his men charged forth and defeated their opponents, who fled in disarray.

After leaving Wales and returning to his capital of Camelot, Arthur found old Merlin waiting for him. It was time, said Merlin, that the young king knew a secret, namely, that his mother, Igraine, wife of Uther Pendragon, was alive. She had been living in seclusion since Uther's death; and because no one had told her what had happened to the infant boy she had given up to Merlin many years before, nor his name, she did not know that the new king was her son. When Merlin brought them together, Igraine and Arthur embraced and wept, and Arthur ordered eight days of feasting to celebrate their reunion.

The Knight of the Fountain

When the eight days had come and gone, a young squire entered Camelot on horseback, leading another steed that bore the dead body of a knight. According to the

Arthur and some of his knights exchange stories of adventure.

squire, he and his master had encountered a formidable knight who had pitched a large tent beside a fountain in the nearby forest; the two knights had fought and the knight of the fountain had emerged the victor. "Might one of Arthur's knights avenge his master?" the squire humbly asked.

At that moment one of Arthur's squires, by the name of Griflet, stepped forward and said to the king, "Sir, I beseech that you make me a knight."[21] Griflet was bent on proving himself worthy of knighthood and offered to challenge the knight of the fountain. Arthur was reluctant at first but soon complied; and the young man, now called *Sir Griflet*, rode out to meet the intruder in the forest.

Possible Location for Camelot

The location of Camelot remains unknown. In her King Arthur, *noted mythologist Norma Goodrich makes the case that Carlisle, in the northern region of Northumbria, was the historical Camelot.*

Carlisle was . . . the second most important Christian center in Britain in Arthur's day, judging from archaeological finds. It was also the . . . most recent Roman capital. Like London, Caerleon, and Chester, it had previously been a *vicus,* or Roman military center. . . . Speaking from a logistical point of view, Carlisle was the kind of center capable of supplying foodstuffs and fodder for many . . . guests, their attendants, and their horses. . . . From the point of view of military security for the king and his guests, Carlisle would have been Arthur's choice. The city is so protected by the natural geography of the land that access by any large number of soldiers would have been extremely difficult. . . . The many road junctions of ancient Carlisle, which may answer to the Arthurian texts' cryptic designation of "the seven roads," would have been protected by Hadrian's Wall [the defensive barrier erected by the Roman emperor Hadrian in the second century A.D.], stretching to the north.

When the knight of the fountain saw the youth approaching, he asked from whence he had come. "I am of Arthur's court"[22] was the reply. The older knight told Sir Griflet to go away, for he was too young and inexperienced to fight a knight as great as himself. But the headstrong Griflet refused to back off and charged the other man, forcing him to defend himself. The knight of the fountain easily unhorsed poor Griflet. But he took pity on him, spared his life, and sent him back to Camelot.

On seeing the wounded Sir Griflet limping into the court, Arthur was filled with rage and ordered that his armor and horse be prepared. Thereupon, the king himself galloped into the forest intent on teaching the knight of the fountain a lesson. Reaching the tent, Arthur gruffly called on the knight to come out and face him, and when the man appeared, the horseman demanded to know who he was. The knight answered that his name was Sir Pellinore. Before long the two men were engaged in a mighty struggle, first with lances on horseback, then with swords and shields on foot. Their swords smashed together with such force, wrote Malory, that

pieces of armor flew into the fields, and much blood they both bled, that all the place in which they fought was overbled with blood. And thus they fought long . . . and hurtled together like two rams . . . [and] the sword of the knight smote Arthur's sword in two pieces.[23]

Having lost his weapon, Arthur leapt through the air, seized Pellinore, and wrestled him to the ground, where the two grappled for several minutes. Finally, Pellinore managed to gain control and raised a dagger to strike. But at that instant Merlin appeared seemingly from nowhere and admonished the knight to stay his hand, for the man he had bested was none other than King Arthur of the Britons. Surprised and ashamed, Pellinore seemed on the verge of slaying himself to make amends for attacking the sovereign; so Merlin cast an enchantment on him, sending him into a deep sleep.

The Lady of the Lake

"Alas," Arthur exclaimed, "what have you done, Merlin? Have you slain this good knight by your magic? There lived no finer knight than he!"

"Do not worry," Merlin replied. "He is but in a sleep, and will awaken within three hours. And hereafter he shall do you right good service and shall have two sons who will be surpassingly good men, one of them the noble Perceval."[24]

Arthur and Merlin set out to reach a mysterious arm bearing a sword, as the Lady of the Lake looks on. The sword was known as Excalibur.

Morgan le Fay

The character of Morgan le Fay, one of Arthur's most treacherous enemies, first appears in Geoffrey of Monmouth's *Life of Merlin,* a short sequel to his *History of the Kings of Britain.* He pictures her as a resident of the mysterious Isle of Avalon, one of nine sisters, skilled in the healing arts, and able to change her shape at will. She may have been based loosely on an ancient goddess, perhaps the Celtic deity Modron (or Matrona) or the Irish Morrigan. In most later Arthurian adaptations, Morgan is related to Arthur; Thomas Malory makes her the daughter of Igraine, wife of Uther Pendragon, and therefore Arthur's half sister. Morgan also routinely appears as queen to Uriens, ruler of the small kingdom of Rheged, and mother of one of Arthur's knights, Sir Uwaine.

As Arthur and Merlin rode away through the forest, the king bemoaned the fact that his trusty sword had been destroyed in the battle. Merlin smiled and told him that he knew of another, far greater sword that would be perfect for Arthur. The old man led the king to a beautiful lake in the midst of the forest, and in the center of the lake, Arthur saw something extraordinary—a woman's arm rising above the water's surface. And in the hand was a magnificent sword.

At that same moment, the king caught sight of a strange young woman dressed all in white on the nearby shore. When Arthur questioned her, she said that she was called the Lady of the Lake; further, she revealed that the sword was called Excalibur, which meant "cut steel." She offered to give Arthur the sword in exchange for a gift of her choosing, which she would name and claim at some future date.

After agreeing to the deal, Arthur found a small barge and used it to reach the center of the lake. There he collected the sword. And immediately the mysterious arm that had held it disappeared beneath the waves. Now that the sword and its scabbard were in Arthur's possession, Merlin informed him that the scabbard had magical properties; as long as the king kept the scabbard close, he would not bleed, no matter how bad the wound.

Hearing this, Arthur decided he must always wield Excalibur in wartime; in times of peace, in contrast, he entrusted the sword and scabbard to his half sister Morgan le Fay, daughter of Igraine, for safekeeping. Little did the young king know that Morgan secretly hated him and would soon attempt to use the weapon against him. Only Merlin, with his prophetic powers, had any inkling of how fraught with danger the future would be for the master of Camelot.

Chapter Three

The Order of the Round Table

Though young King Arthur had managed to unite much of England under his banner, a few powerful lords in Wales and elsewhere remained independent and aloof. At least they did not for the moment pose a danger to the realm, Arthur reasoned. On the other hand, in the north the Scots and Picts periodically raided and pillaged English villages and farms; and the foreign Saxons remained a threat, as every few years they launched an invasion across the English Channel. Sometimes they stayed for months or even years on English soil, and it required Herculean efforts to dislodge them.

The War with the Saxons

Arthur became determined to deal with these enemies of law, order, and chivalry. A few years into his reign, he and his soldiers met a combined army of Scots, Picts, and Saxons near the Douglas River and soundly defeated them. A month or so later, in another battle between the Britons and Saxons, the latter fled from Arthur's forces. According to Geoffrey of Monmouth:

> Arthur pursued the Saxons relentlessly until they reached Caledon Wood. There they reformed [their battle line] after their flight and made an effort to resist Arthur. The Saxons joined battle once more and killed a number of the Britons. . . . They used the shelter of the trees to protect themselves from the Britons' weapons. As soon as Arthur saw this, he ordered the trees round that part of the wood to be cut down and their trunks to be placed in a circle,

Arthur and his troops defeat the Saxons at Mount Badon. According to the legends, his victory kept the Saxons out of England for the rest of his reign.

so that every way out was barred to the enemy. Arthur's plan was to hem them in and then besiege them, so that in the end they should die of hunger. When this had been done, he ordered his squadrons to surround the wood and there he remained for three days. The Saxons had nothing to eat. To prevent themselves [from] dying of sheer hunger, they asked permission to come out, on the understanding that, if they left behind all their gold and silver, they might be permitted to return to Germany with nothing but their boats.[25]

After consulting with his most trusted knights, Arthur, who was as merciful as he was formidable in dealing with opponents, decided to accept the deal the Saxons had proposed. He allowed them safe passage to the coast, where they embarked on their ships. However, before they had reached the shores of Gaul, they decided to go back on their word; they turned their vessels around, sailed back to England, ravaged the coast, and then marched overland to Bath, near Mount Badon. There they besieged the town and caused much destruction and misery.

On hearing of the Saxons' treachery, Arthur immediately regrouped his army and led it on a forced march toward Bath. After making camp near the besieged town, the king stood on a tall rock and addressed his troops, saying:

Although the Saxons, whose very name is an insult to heaven and detested by all men, have not kept faith with me, I myself will keep faith with my God. This very day I will do my utmost to take vengeance on them for the blood of my fellow countrymen. Arm yourselves, men, and attack those traitors with all your strength! With Christ's help, we shall conquer them, without any possible doubt![26]

Then Arthur donned a splendid leather jerkin and golden helmet topped by a crest carved in the image of a dragon. Grasping Excalibur, still resting within its magical scabbard, he chose a circular shield bearing the painted likeness of the Virgin Mary and strode to the forefront of his army. In a loud voice, the king gave the order to attack the Saxons, who had formed a battle line near the slopes of Mount Badon; and the two armies came together amidst a terrible din of crashing metal and raised voices. All day long the bloody struggle raged, until Arthur and his men gained the upper hand. Once again the Saxons fled, this time never to return in Arthur's lifetime.

Arthur Versus the Visigoths?

Historian Geoffrey Ashe has proposed that Arthur's legendary military exploits against barbarian hordes may be based on the exploits of a real fifth-century British king, Riothamus. In his Discovery of King Arthur, *Ashe quotes a sixth-century chronicler, Jordanes, who reported:*

[The eastern Roman emperor] Leo chose as emperor [in the West] his patrician Anthemius and sent him to Rome. . . . Now Euric, king of the Visigoths, perceived the frequent changes of Roman emperors and strove to hold Gaul in his own right. The emperor Anthemius heard of it and asked the Britons for aid. Their king Riothamus came with twelve thousand men into the state of Bituriges by way of the ocean, and was received as he disembarked from his ships. . . . Euric came against them with an innumerable army, and after a long fight he routed Riothamus, before the Romans could join him. . . . When he [Riothamus] had lost a great part of his army, he fled with all the men he could gather together.

The Fair Guinevere

It was not long after Arthur's defeat of the Saxons that some of his knights began to advise him to take a wife. A man of his noble and heroic stature should create an heir of the same stature, they said, so that the realm would be in good hands when the day finally came that the king passed on. In addition, a queen would bring an air of warmth, grace, polish, and manners into a court dominated by fighting men, who so often care little for such niceties.

The young Guinevere, daughter of King Leodegrance of Cameliard.

When Arthur told Merlin what the knights had counseled, the old magician agreed. "It is well done," said Merlin (according to Malory), "that you take a wife, for a man of your bounty and nobility should not be without a wife. Now, is there any fair lady that you love better than another?"

"Yes," said Arthur, "I love Guinevere, King Leodegrance's daughter, of the land of Cameliard. This damsel is the gentlest and fairest lady that I know living, or yet that ever I could find."[27] Arthur explained how he had met Guinevere on several occasions when he had visited her father to plan strategy against their mutual enemies.

When Merlin heard Arthur praise the fair Guinevere, his expression changed. He possessed the gift of prophecy, of course; and though he could not foresee the exact unfolding of future events, something within him warned that unhappiness would come of a union between Arthur and Guinevere. Yet Merlin did not reveal this uneasy feeling to the king. The old man loved Arthur as his own son and could not bring himself to keep the young man from following the dictates of his heart.

So Merlin journeyed to the land of Cameliard and informed King Leodegrance that King Arthur wished to marry young Guinevere. "That is to me the best tidings that ever I heard," Leodegrance exclaimed with joy, "that so worthy a king of prowess and of nobility will wed my daughter."[28] And the goodly king commended Guinevere into the keeping of Merlin, who led her back to Arthur. When the young woman entered the great hall, Arthur eagerly, but respectfully took her hand; and in Malory's version, before all present he announced, "This fair lady is wonderfully welcome to me, for I have loved her long, and therefore there is nothing so pleasing to me."[29]

The Round Table

At the king's order, preparations began for the wedding and Guinevere's coronation as queen. The pomp and ceremony was to be all the greater, he publicly proclaimed, for at the same time the kingdom would celebrate the establishment of a new order of knighthood and chivalry in the land. Ever since ascending the throne, Arthur had demanded that his knights behave honorably; they were to refrain from bullying and otherwise misusing the common people, which had been common before his reign, and to use their superior strength and status for the public good. But he had long dreamed of finding a way to make this policy more formal and permanent, to establish standards of decency and goodness not only in his own time but for all ages to come.

Now a way to accomplish this goal had seemingly presented itself. Many years before, Arthur's father, Uther Pendragon, had given a large round dining table made of the finest oak to King Leodegrance as a wedding present. And when Merlin visited Leodegrance to ask

A sixteenth-century engraving depicts Arthur (center) and his knights.

for Guinevere's hand, the aging king decided to return the favor for the next generation. "I shall send Arthur a gift that shall please him," he told Merlin, "for I shall give him the Table Round, the one Uther Pendragon gave me."[30] The table was so large, Leodegrance said, that as many as 150 knights could sit around it at one time.

On receiving this most unusual gift, Arthur suddenly realized how it could become the cornerstone of his new order of chivalry. Though he did not have enough noble knights to fill all the seats around the table, he could search for more, some even from faraway lands. This would create ties of friendship with those lands. Moreover, the table's very shape inspired equality and comradeship rather than jealousy and rivalry. As one Arthurian chronicler put it:

The Winchester Round Table

A number of towns in Britain claim to own Arthur's Round Table or at least fragments of it. One of the most famous is the Winchester Round Table, which now rests in the great hall of Winchester Castle, southeast of London. Sir Thomas Malory identified Winchester with Camelot; and his publisher, William Caxton, and others in his day were convinced that the table, which is eighteen feet in diameter and made of oak, was really Arthur's. Accepting this view, Caxton's contemporary King Henry VII (reigned 1485–1509) sought to use the table to enhance the image of the royal family. He took his pregnant wife to Winchester, and there she gave birth to a son, whom they named Arthur II. But Henry's hopes of uniting England in a new Arthurian age were dashed when the child died prematurely in 1502.

This Round Table was ordained of Arthur that when his fair fellowship [of knights] sat [around it] . . . their chairs should be alike, their service equal, and none [ranked] before or after his comrade. Thus no man could boast that he was exalted above his fellow, for all alike were gathered round the board, and none were alien at the breaking of Arthur's bread.[31]

In the Service of Good

To fill the empty seats at the table, Arthur sent Merlin and others out in every direction to invite the strongest and noblest knights to join the new fellowship. Only those who would agree to use their might in the service of good, rather than to impose their will on others, were welcome, Arthur decreed. "In this way," another chronicler remarked,

he developed such a code of courtliness in his household that he inspired peoples living far away to imitate him. The result was that even the man of noblest birth . . . thought nothing of himself unless he wore his arms and dressed in the same way as Arthur's knights. At last the fame of Arthur's generosity and bravery spread to the very ends of the earth.[32]

Furthermore, both old and new knights swore an oath to uphold the honor of the fellowship, to aid damsels or others who were sorely oppressed or otherwise in danger or distress, and at all times to live by the rules of law and justice.

When all but three of the seats of the Round Table had been filled with worthy knights, there arrived at Camelot young

Gawain, son of King Lot of Orkney. Because King Lot's queen was Morgause, Arthur's half sister, Gawain was Arthur's nephew. The goodly Gawain requested that the king knight him and allow him to sit at the Round Table, and Arthur readily agreed. That left two empty seats. Then Merlin arrived with Sir Pellinore, the knight of the fountain, who had sparred with Arthur in the forest a few years before. Arthur extended his hand, told Pellinore there were no hard feelings about the past, and invited him to join the fellowship. Relieved at the chance to make amends with the king, Pellinore took Arthur's hand, swore the knightly oath, and seated himself at the table.

Now only one empty seat remained. When Arthur optimistically predicted they would be able to fill it soon, Merlin warned that they must not do so. This was the Siege Perilous, the "Seat of Danger," he explained. It must remain vacant until the arrival of a knight whose purity of heart and mind was second to none. Before that day, every man who might dare to sit in the seat would be instantly swallowed up by the earth, never to be seen again.

The Magic Ship

In the years that followed, the order of the Round Table maintained justice in the country, just as Arthur had intended.

The knights of the fellowship of the Round Table, seen here renewing their oath to Arthur, enforced justice throughout the land.

The Hot-Tempered Sir Gawain

Sir Gawain, the excellent knight who appears in the Arthurian legends as Arthur's nephew, was based on a character named Gwalchmei in the old Welsh tales and Walwanus in Geoffrey of Monmouth's History of the Kings of Britain. *According to Christopher Snyder in his* World of King Arthur, *Gawain*

is usually depicted as being courteous and well-mannered, making him attractive to the ladies, a mixed blessing and cause of many of his adventures (and misadventures). His great strength was, curiously, said to increase until noonday and decrease with the setting of the sun, while his hot temper led him into frequent feuds. His sometimes violent nature prevented him from achieving the Holy Grail, though he was the first to vow to make the quest. In some romances he marries a woman named Ragnell, and his sons appear occasionally as Round Table knights.

Adhering to their oath, the knights helped the meek and oppressed, as well as one another when danger threatened. Yet deceit and treachery still lingered in the land, though most of those who practiced these ills were careful to do so in secret.

Arthur learned this sad fact in a very personal way when his half sister the enchantress (witch or sorceress) Morgan le Fay attempted to use his special sword, Excalibur, to kill him and further her own twisted aims. Not realizing she hated him with a vengeance, he had entrusted her to safeguard the weapon in peacetime. And taking advantage of this trust, she hatched an evil plan. Though she was married to King Uriens, of the land of Rheged, she had a secret lover—Sir Accolon of Gaul, who had recently become a knight of the Round Table. Morgan hoped to place Accolon on Arthur's throne and make

herself queen of the Britons. Accolon knew that his lover wanted to get rid of the king, whom he respected, and in his heart he felt he should warn Arthur. But Accolon was weaker-willed than Morgan and in her power, so he reluctantly kept silent.

The evil plot unfolded in the following way. Morgan arranged for Arthur, Uriens, and Accolon to go hunting together in a deep forest. When they had chased their prey for many hours, they came to a large lake and saw a small ship at anchor near the shore. The king said that they should go and investigate the contents of the ship. Inside, the men found twelve beautiful maidens, who knelt before the king, called him by name, and invited him and his companions to rest there for the night. Each man was led to a comfortable, richly decorated chamber, where, thanks to the exertions of the day, he fell asleep almost at once.

Then a very strange thing happened. When the men awoke the next morning, they found themselves in strange, unexpected places rather than on the ship. Uriens was at Camelot with his wife, Morgan le Fay; Arthur woke up in a dark dungeon; and Accolon lay beside a deep well in an unknown wood. This trickery was Morgan's doing, of course; for the ship had been only an illusion designed to put Arthur and Accolon on a deadly collision course.

Arthur's half sister, Morgan le Fay.

The Warring Brothers

When Arthur awoke in the prison cell, he saw twenty knights lying chained, unwashed, and very thin for lack of food. He learned that they had been languishing in the cell for a long time, some for as many as seven years. And when he inquired why and how they had come to this pitiful state, they answered:

> The lord of this castle is named Sir Damas, and he is the falsest knight alive, and full of treason, and the worst coward that ever lived. He has a younger brother, a good knight of prowess, named Sir Ontzlake, and this traitor, Sir Damas, the elder brother, will give him no part of his heritage. . . . Great war has been waged between them . . . and Ontzlake keeps offering Damas to fight for the heritage, and if he will not do it himself, to find a knight to fight *for* him. Unto this Sir Damas agreed, but he is so hated that there is never a knight who will fight for him. Seeing this, Damas has . . . taken all the other knights in this country separately by force . . . and brought them to this prison.[33]

The chained knights explained further that Damas had promised to let any man out of the dungeon who would agree to fight for him against his brother, Ontzlake; but all had refused, and that was why they remained captive.

No sooner had the knights finished their story when a young woman appeared at the cell door. She motioned to Arthur to come near, and she told him that if he would fight for her father, the lord of this castle, he would win his freedom. Arthur did not want to fight for a wicked lord like Damas. But he felt an obligation to help the twenty poor and bedraggled knights escape their predicament; so he told the maiden that he would agree to fight on the condition that the twenty knights in the cell with him would be set free.

What Arthur did not know was that the maiden was not Damas's daughter, but actually a handmaiden of the double-dealing Morgan le Fay. The maiden went to Damas and told him Arthur had agreed to fight for him; and Damas agreed to Arthur's demand, promising to free him and the other knights after Arthur defeated Ontzlake. Damas did not realize that he, too, was the victim of treachery, for Morgan had arranged it so that Arthur would lose the battle.

The Real and False Excaliburs

This part of Morgan's scheme becomes clear when one considers the situation in which Sir Accolon found himself when he woke up beside the well in the woods. "Heaven save my lord King Arthur and King Uriens," he said (in Malory's words), "for these damsels in the ship have betrayed us. They were demons, and no women, and if I escape this mis-

adventure, I shall destroy all false damsels who use enchantment."[34]

At that moment a dwarf appeared and said he had been sent by Morgan le Fay. "She greets you well," the dwarf told Accolon,

and bids you to be strong of heart, for you shall fight tomorrow with a knight at the hour of noon, and therefore she has sent you here Excalibur, Arthur's sword, and the scabbard. She bids you, as you love her, that you do battle to the utmost, without any mercy.[35]

The real Excalibur. The tricky Morgan le Fay presented Arthur with a fake.

Grasping Excalibur, Accolon made his way through the forest until he met up with a knight, who turned out to be none other than Sir Ontzlake, Damas's brother. Ontzlake told Accolon that he was on his way to fight Damas's champion, despite the fact that he, Ontzlake, was suffering mightily from some wounds sustained in an earlier battle. Having pledged to help fellow knights in need, Accolon offered to fight in the other man's place and rode away toward the fateful meeting.

Meanwhile, at Damas's castle, another of Morgan le Fay's handmaidens brought a sword and scabbard to Arthur, saying that this was his trusty Excalibur. In reality, though, it was a much inferior replica. This became clear to Arthur once the combat with Accolon had begun. Arthur did not realize whom he was fighting, nor did Accolon; Morgan had seen to that by casting a spell over them. But Arthur saw that he was bleeding profusely, while his opponent had not a single scratch, even though Arthur had struck him hard numerous times. Somehow, Arthur knew, the Excalibur he held was false, while his attacker held the real one.

This suspicion was confirmed after Arthur managed to retrieve the real Excalibur and thereby gain the upper hand. As Malory wrote, standing over his fallen opponent, the king demanded, "Now tell me, or I will slay you, of what country are you from, and what court?"

"Sir Knight," said Sir Accolon, "I am of the court of King Arthur, and my name is Accolon of Gaul."[36]

Greatly surprised, Arthur demanded to know more, and Accolon admitted knowing that his lover, Morgan, wanted to murder the king. "But that is now done," said Accolon, "for I am sure of my death. But now that I have told you the truth, I pray you tell me who you are and of what court?"

"O, Accolon," said Arthur, "I am King Arthur, to whom you have done great damage."

When Accolon heard that, he cried aloud: "Fair sweet lord, have mercy on me for I knew you not!"

"Mercy you shall have, Sir Accolon," said Arthur, "because I see that just now you knew not who I was. But I understand well by your words that you have agreed to my death and therefore are a traitor; but I blame you the less, for my sister, Morgan le Fay, by her false crafts made you agree and consent to her wickedness."[37]

Thereupon, Arthur ordered the twenty imprisoned knights released and instructed Sir Damas, on pain of death, to give his brother, Sir Ontzlake, his rightful inheritance. As for Sir Accolon, though spared by good-hearted Arthur, he died of his wounds shortly afterward. Arthur sent some knights ahead to Camelot to tell Morgan le Fay that her lover was dead and also that the real Excalibur was once more in the king's possession. Thus did the first attempt to topple Arthur and his new order fail. In the fullness of time, there would be others.

Chapter Four

THE COMING OF LANCELOT

It came to pass that one of the knights who heard about and was determined to join the order of the Round Table was Lancelot du Lac, the eldest son of King Ban of Benwick, in France. The title "du Lac," meaning "of the lake," derived from the fact that as a child Lancelot had been tutored by the Lady of the Lake, just as Arthur had been by his own mentor, Merlin. Supplementing what he had learned from the Lady about the natural world, Lancelot applied himself rigorously to training in weapons use and chivalry; and by the age of eighteen, he was already the most skilled warrior in France.

Widely circulated stories of the adventures of the noble knights who followed King Arthur in Britain inspired Lancelot. In fact, it would not be inaccurate to say that the impressionable young prince worshiped Arthur well before he met him. In

Lancelot's view, a man who could defeat the Saxons, unite the British lords and kings, and initiate a new era of chivalry and justice had to be the greatest hero of them all; and the young man could think of no higher calling than to journey to Camelot and offer his services to this king of earthly kings. Lancelot could not at that moment have foreseen that he would one day become the greatest of all Arthur's knights; nor that his love for the king's wife would contribute to the collapse of the knightly order he so admired.

Battle with the Black Knight

As Lancelot left Benwick Castle, crossed the English Channel, and made his way across southern England, he rehearsed over and over again in his mind the words he might say to Arthur at their first meeting. The young man prayed that he would not be too nervous and perhaps stumble in his speech, thereby making a bad first impression. As it turned out, the nature of that fateful first meeting was quite different than Lancelot had imagined; and the impression he made was very far from bad.

The incident occurred in the following manner. Near the end of his journey, Lancelot came into a clearing in a forest and saw a knight dressed in black armor sitting atop a magnificent horse. The black knight's visor was closed and his shield was masked by canvas so that his blazon (shield crest) was not visible; thus, there was no way to identify him. Lancelot had a gut feeling that the other man wanted to fight him. This impression was verified when the black knight raised his lance and pointed it menacingly toward the center of the clearing; clearly, he was challenging the young Frenchman to a joust.

Never one to run from a fight, Lancelot steered his horse to the appointed spot and prepared for battle. "The two knights faced each other from opposite ends of the little glade," one Arthurian storyteller put it. "Then, although neither of them had so far spoken a word, they . . . put spurs to their horses and began to charge."[38] Lancelot had been in hundreds of jousts. But never before had he actually been in a fight to the death, as he was certain he was now. So as he bore down on his opponent, he concentrated with all his might on the lessons he had learned in his training. At the crucial moment, this training paid off for Lancelot.

The point of his spear took the black knight under the rim of his shoulder-harness at exactly the right place. His mount was in full gallop, and the black knight's was still in a cantor. The black knight and his horse . . . left the ground together . . . and came down again with a crash. As Lancelot rode by, he could see them sprawling on the ground together, with the knight's broken lance between the horse's legs and one flashing horseshoe tearing the canvas from the fallen shield.[39]

Four queens find Lancelot sleeping in this famous painting by Frank C. Cooper.

As the canvas came off, Lancelot saw the blazon beneath and suddenly recognized it as the symbol of King Arthur, which was by this time world-renowned. All at once it dawned on the young man that he had nearly killed the man he respected most in the world. Shocked and mortified, Lancelot jumped down from his steed, rushed to the fallen knight, knelt, and bowed his head. He began to beg for Arthur's forgiveness. But the king, who was struggling to

An eighteenth-century illustration shows Lancelot courting Guinevere.

remove his helmet, would have none of it. Arthur explained that he had heard Lancelot was on his way to Camelot and thought it would be fun to test his skill with the lance. It had been a magnificent joust, Arthur exclaimed; Lancelot had acquitted himself amazingly well and had nothing to be sorry for.

The Wicked Sir Melvas

Once back at Camelot, Arthur formally knighted Lancelot. All of the original seats at the Round Table were full by this time, but Arthur saw that new ones were added for those knights who proved themselves worthy enough, as Lancelot certainly had. As an added gesture, Arthur gave a castle—Joyous Gard, located in northern Britain—to the new knight. And the king introduced Lancelot to Queen Guinevere, who extended her hand for the young Frenchman to kiss in courtly fashion. At first, she did not think Lancelot any more remarkable than the many other knights in Arthur's entourage. But as the months went by, as Malory wrote, she came to hold "him in great favor above all other knights, and certainly he loved the queen above all other ladies and damsels all the days of his life, and for her he did many great deeds of arms, and saved her . . . through his noble chivalry."[40]

One of the most noteworthy of these deeds was Lancelot's role in the rescue of the queen after she had been abducted by a wicked knight known as Sir Melvas. The trouble began when Melvas, arrayed in his most impressive armor, suddenly

An Early Version of Guinevere's Abduction

One of the first literary references to the abduction of Guinevere by Sir Melvas was in the Life of Gildas *(ca. 1155 or before), by Caradoc of Llancarfan. In this early version of the story, a local cleric and the British chronicler Gildas, rather than Lancelot or Arthur, win the queen's release.*

Glastonbury was besieged by . . . Arthur with an enormous army, on account of Guinevere his wife, who had been snatched away and raped by . . . wicked King Melvas and taken to Glastonbury. . . . [Arthur] had been searching everywhere for the queen for an entire year, and had at last discovered her whereabouts. . . . The abbot of Glastonbury, together with . . . Gildas the Wise, entered the battlefield and advised Melvas to make peace with his king and restore the captive queen. So she was returned, as she should have been, peacefully and in good faith.

and boldly appeared in the court at Camelot. "King Arthur," he said to the king in an insolent tone (in Chrétien de Troyes's version),

I hold in captivity knights, ladies, and maidens from your land and your household. However, I give you this news of them not because I intend to return them to you. On the contrary, I wish to tell and inform you that you lack the strength and resources to be able to get them back. And you can be sure you'll die without ever being in a position to help them.[41]

Arthur was sorely grieved to learn both that his people were in captivity and that another adversary had arisen to chal-lenge his rule and realm. He was about to demand that the intruder release the prisoners when Sir Melvas spoke again:

King, if there is in your court so much as one knight whom you trust enough to dare hand over to him the queen, to be taken after me into those woods where I'm heading, I'll promise to wait for him there; and if he can win her from me and manage to bring her back, I'll return to you all the prisoners held captive in my land.[42]

Having said this, the arrogant Sir Melvas departed, leaving the court abuzz with worry and anticipation. Almost immediately, Arthur's brother, Sir Kay, stepped forward and volunteered to take up the wicked knight's challenge. Arthur was reluctant to allow him to go, not to mention to take Guinevere with him; after all, if Sir Melvas was actually able to defeat Kay, Guinevere would be in Melvas's power along with the other hostages. But Kay adamantly insisted he would emerge the winner, so the king consented and watched his brother and wife ride away into the forest.

The Knight of the Cart

As it turned out, Arthur should have trusted his first instinct. Employing deceit and unscrupulous tactics, Melvas defeated Kay and carried the frightened Guinevere away. Hearing this appalling news, Arthur and Gawain immediately gathered their weapons and rode off in pursuit. As the two men moved along the road that led northward toward Melvas's domain, another mounted knight, wearing an outfit that concealed his identity, suddenly passed them at a tremendous clip. Arthur remarked to Gawain that this fellow was pushing his horse too hard; the exertion would likely kill it. Sure enough, a few hours later Arthur and Gawain found the unknown knight's horse sprawled dead on the side of the road. The owner was nowhere in sight.

Eventually, the king and his companion reached Melvas's castle, where they fully expected to fight a battle to the death to save the queen. Instead, they were surprised to find Melvas lying dead and Guinevere and the other hostages free and safe. Some eyewitnesses told

Arthur that a knight, whose face had been well hidden, had caught up to Sir Melvas and his captive just as they were approaching the castle. The mysterious knight was driving not a horse but a wooden cart, the witness said. Leaping from the cart, the knight had engaged Melvas in furious hand-to-hand combat and slain him; then the victorious knight had freed the other hostages, saluted the queen, and disappeared as quickly as he had come.

Guinevere knew the truth, namely, that the knight of the cart was Sir Lancelot. He had concealed his identity so as to divert suspicion from his secret relationship with the queen. After riding his poor horse to death, he had commandeered a peasant's cart to complete the journey and had luckily arrived in the nick of time. The rescue had demonstrated his devotion to Guinevere and made her love him all the more.

What both Guinevere and Lancelot did not know was that Arthur was not fooled by the masquerade. He had long suspected what was happening behind his back; but out of love for his wife and friend, as well as a greatness of spirit beyond that of normal men, he had chosen to remain silent. Sitting alone in his throne room after he and Guinevere had returned to Camelot, he said (in Alan Jay Lerner's version):

If I could choose from every woman who breathes on this earth, the face I would most love [would be Guinevere's]. . . . If I could choose from every man who breathes on this earth [he would be Lancelot]. . . . Yes, I love them, and they answer me with pain and torment . . . and [as a man I feel that] they must pay for it and be punished. . . . [But] I'm a king, not a [mere] man. And a civilized king. Could it possibly be civilized to destroy what I love? . . . What of *their* pain and torment? Did they ask for this calamity? Can passion be selected? . . . [Raising his sword] By God, Excalibur, I shall be a king! This is the time of King Arthur . . . and violence is not strength and compassion is not weakness. We shall live through this together, Excalibur: They, you, and I! And God have mercy on us all.[43]

The love between Lancelot and Guinevere was doomed from the start, as it broke the Arthurian code of chivalry.

The Coming of Sir Galahad

Arthur's feelings about Lancelot and Guinevere's relationship aside, by loving another man's wife, Lancelot had broken the Arthurian code of chivalry. And this mistake ended up keeping him from achieving the greatest goal ever sought by any of Arthur's knights—finding and holding the sacred Holy Grail.

The immediate events leading up to the memorable quest for the cup of Christ began when King Arthur received a message from his old mentor, Merlin. The Grail was hidden somewhere in Britain, the magician reported. Only a person of truly pure heart and soul could find it and in doing so cleanse the Britons of their past sins; moreover, the man destined to find the Grail was alive at that very moment and Arthur would soon meet him.

Excited by Merlin's words, Arthur wondered how he might discern the identity of the person destined to seek out the Grail. But that information came to him in a way he did not anticipate. Camelot was then preparing its annual celebration of the Pentecost (a feast commemorating the seventh Sunday after Easter, when Christ appeared to the apostles). No sooner had the Pentecost come and the feast

In an illustration from an old Italian manuscript, Galahad appears at Arthur's court.

no mortal hand was seen to bear it. ... It circled the hall along the great tables and each place was furnished in its wake with the food its occupants desired. When all were served, the Holy Grail vanished, they knew not how or where.[44]

After the vision had ended, Arthur and his guests regained the power of speech and all agreed that the kingdom had been given a special honor. Sir Gawain cried out that he would gladly go on a quest to find the sacred cup and never rest until he had found it. Numerous other knights sprang to their feet and offered similar vows. And suddenly Arthur was troubled, for he realized that the loss of so many of his strongest knights to such a quest would break up the glorious fellowship of the Round Table, which he had labored so long to achieve.

Before the king could muse further, he heard a new flurry of voices arise and saw that everyone was looking toward the front of the hall. An old hermit was leading an extraordinarily handsome young man through the crowd and toward the throne. The hermit told Arthur that the young man was Galahad, the son of Sir Lancelot, news that caught everyone present by surprise. Galahad had been raised by his mother, Elaine, at the court of his grandfather, King Ban, in France, the hermit continued. And he had come to Camelot to prove his worth as a knight of the Round Table.

begun, when all the noble knights and ladies who had gathered in the castle's great hall witnessed a singular and wondrous event. As described in the anonymous *Quest of the Holy Grail:*

There came a clap of thunder so loud and terrible that they thought the palace must fall. Suddenly the hall was lit by a sunbeam which shed a radiance through the palace seven times brighter than had been seen before. ... Not one of those present could utter a word, for all had been struck dumb. ... When they had sat a long while thus, unable to speak and gazing at one another like dumb animals, the Holy Grail appeared, covered with a cloth of white. ... Yet

Requesting that everyone watch closely, the old man led Galahad around the great Round Table to the Siege Perilous, which had remained conspicuously vacant since the table's founding. Everyone expected that when Galahad sat there, he would vanish into the depths. But to their astonishment, he sat in the seat without ill effect. Seeing this, Arthur declared that Galahad was indeed welcome in Camelot, for the Seat of Danger had obviously been intended for him alone.

The Quest for the Grail

But Galahad was not destined to occupy his seat at the Round Table for long. As many other knights had earlier, he now pledged to go in search of the sacred Grail. In a sad voice, Arthur told his assembled knights that he feared this might be the last time he would see them all together as a fellowship of brave comrades. So the following day they should have one last tournament and joust together to celebrate that fellowship and their friendship. Fulfilling this request, the next morning all the knights met in the jousting area in a meadow near the castle.

Not long after the tournament, Sir Galahad, Sir Gawain, Sir Perceval, Sir Lancelot, and several other knights set out, each in a different direction, to seek the Holy Grail. As it turned out, most of these knights did not fare well. Sir Gawain, for example, early realized that he was not pure enough of heart to be

Arthur Laments His Knights' Departure

In this beautifully written speech from the anonymous Quest of the Holy Grail, *Arthur expresses to Sir Gawain that the upcoming quests for the Grail will have a negative effect on the fellowship of the Round Table.*

Ah, Gawain, this vow of yours is a mortal blow to me, for you have deprived me of the best and truest companions a man could find. I speak of the fellowship of the Round Table, for I am well aware that those who leave my court when the hour comes, all will not return. On the contrary, many shall fall in this quest, and success will not come so swiftly as you think. This saddens me not a little. I have raised them up and advanced them to the utmost of my power, and have always loved them and indeed love them still like sons or brothers; how should I not grieve at their departure? I have grown accustomed to their presence and have learned to like their company; I cannot find in me the strength to bear the loss.

worthy of seeing the sacred cup; so he gave up and returned to Camelot.

As for Lancelot, though he was uncommonly brave, the moral stain of his love affair with the queen had made him unworthy of beholding and touching the Grail. For many months he journeyed far and wide, following every lead. And once he actually came within a mere few yards of the coveted artifact. A strange voice told him to enter a castle, and when he did so, he saw through an open door a magnificent altar decorated with priceless silver and gold. Lancelot could sense that the Grail was in that chamber; and though the voice told him not to enter, he ignored the warning. However, Malory wrote, as he stepped through the door,

Arthur's knights receive a blessing from the archbishop of Canterbury before leaving on their various quests to find the elusive Holy Grail.

Sir Galahad Completes His Quest

In this excerpt from Thomas Malory's Le Morte d'Arthur *(Sidney Lanier's edition), Sir Galahad is transformed by the fabulous Holy Grail.*

Now Sir Galahad rode many journeys in vain, and afterward, meeting with Sir Bors and Sir Perceval, they knew many wonders and adventures; till on a certain day they came down into a ship, and in the midst thereof they found a table of silver and the Holy Grail all covered with white samite [silk]. And the Holy Grail wrought many miracles, comforting them in prison, feeding them, and healing the sick....[They traveled to Jerusalem, where] on a certain morning Sir Galahad went into the palace and saw before him the Holy Grail, and a man kneeling and a great fellowship of angels. Then Sir Galahad knew his hour had come. And he went to Sir Perceval and Sir Bors and kissed them and commended them to God....And therewith he kneeled down before the table and made his prayers; and suddenly his soul departed, and a great multitude of angels bore his soul up to heaven. Also, Perceval and Bors saw come from heaven a hand, but they saw not the body; and then it came to the Holy Grail and took it ...and bore it to heaven.

he felt a breath of air as if it were mixed with fire, and it smote him so sore in the face that it seemed to burn him, and therewith he fell to the earth, and had no power to rise. Then he felt about him many hands, which took him up and bore him out of the chamber, and left him seemingly dead. And on the morrow he was found by the people of the castle outside the chamber door. Four-and-twenty days Sir Lancelot lay as if dead, but on the twenty-fifth day he opened his eyes. . . . He knew now that his quest was ended, that he would never see . . . the Holy Grail.[45]

Lancelot returned to Camelot, where Arthur and Guinevere happily welcomed him home. None spoke of the reason for his failure, but all knew the truth in their hearts. In a way it was a sad homecoming, for Lancelot learned that in the time he had been away, more than half the knights of the Round Table had been slain either while searching for the Grail or in other adventures. "Now I would to God," said Arthur in a sorrowful voice (in Malory's version), "that they were all here."

"That shall never be,"[46] Lancelot responded just as sadly.

Meanwhile, it was Galahad who finally found the holy chalice. In faraway Jerusalem, where the cup's original owner had been crucified long before, that knight had finally held the fabulous artifact in his hands. He had bidden a touching farewell to his companions, Sir Perceval and Sir Bors. And a choir of angels had borne him in a blaze of glory into heaven, leaving Arthur, the queen, and her lover behind to face the most ominous threat Camelot had yet faced.

Chapter Five

THE TREACHERY OF MORDRED

Though Arthur had devoted his life to the order of the Round Table and the creation of a realm built on principles of brotherhood, kindness, and justice, he could not stop the chaotic and evil forces that worked to undermine his efforts. The first major setback had been the loss of so many of the knights who had departed in search of the Holy Grail. This blow to the Round Table had at least been motivated by a devout desire to do good and to serve God faithfully. Furthermore, it had left the fellowship of knights intact, if damaged. Much worse, and indeed ultimately fatal to the Arthurian order, was a conscious attempt by men consumed by ambition, greed, and jealousy to undermine its foundations.

The seeds of this disaster had been planted long before, and their malignant roots had been growing and spreading, quiet and unseen, ever since. Back when Arthur's kingship was still new and fresh and filled with optimism, Merlin had come to him one day with a dark

Arthur and the Grail are pictured in this fifteenth-century illustration.

Haunted by a Youthful Mistake

In this excerpt from T. H. White's Once and Future King, *the middle-aged Arthur laments to Lancelot and Guinevere about the time in his youth when he sent away the male children born on May Day.*

I was young, I was nineteen. And Merlin came, too late, to say what had happened. Everybody told me what a dreadful sin it was, and how nothing but sorrow would come of it. . . . They frightened me with horrible prophecies, and I did something which has haunted me ever since. . . . I let them make a proclamation that all the children born at a certain time were to be put in a big ship and floated out to sea. I wanted to destroy Mordred for his own sake, and I didn't know where he would be born. . . . The ship was floated off, and Mordred was on it, and it was wrecked on an island. Most of the poor babies were drowned—but God saved Mordred, and sent him back to shame me afterwards.

prophecy. One day far in the future, the old man had said, much evil would befall Arthur's Britain, for a male child born on the first day of May would grow up to cause the fall of both Arthur and the fellowship of the Round Table.

Hearing this ominous tiding, Arthur had been hard-pressed to find a way to avert such calamitous events. For the good of the kingdom and its future, he decided it would be best to send away all male children born on May Day. He ordered that they be put on a ship and taken across the English Channel, where new homes would be found for them in Europe. Unfortunately, a violent storm blew up and wrecked the ship in mid-journey. And all but one of the children perished. But the boy who survived and washed ashore was the very one that Merlin's prophecy had foreseen; he was Mordred, son of the wife of King Lot of Orkney and King Arthur's own nephew. A kindly man found the shipwrecked boy and raised him until he was a teenager. Then he brought him to the royal court, where Mordred eventually became a knight of the Round Table. Neither Arthur nor anyone else realized that this restless young man would, in the fullness of time, bring ruin and misery to all concerned.

A Serious Accusation

When Mordred finally felt confident that the time was right to make trouble for Arthur and begin the process of usurping the throne, the mischievous knight sought to enlist the aid of other knights. First he approached his half brothers— Sir Gawain, Sir Gaheris, and Sir Gareth (who were all sons of King Lot). For a long time rumors had spun around the court of the illicit love shared by Queen Guinevere and Sir Lancelot behind the king's back, said Mordred. Surely these rumors were based on fact, he continued, and it was time that they show enough courage to step forward and formally denounce the queen and her lover to Arthur.

But Gawain and the others were loath to hurl such damning accusations at the queen. According to Malory,

Sir Gareth (in foreground) was one of Mordred's half brothers. Gareth was among the several knights slain during Lancelot's rescue of Guinevere.

Gawain said, "I pray you and charge you to speak no more of such things before me, for I will not be of your counsel."

"Truly," said Gaheris and Gareth in agreement, "we will have nothing to do with your deeds."

"Mordred," Gawain added, "I wish you would drop this matter, and not make yourself such a busybody, for I know what will come of it. For if there arise war between Sir Lancelot and us, many great lords will hold with Sir Lancelot. And for my part I will never be against Sir Lancelot."[47]

What support Mordred lost from his brothers he soon gained from a disgrun-

Ladies of the court spread the rumor about the affair between Guinevere and Lancelot (foreground). Eventually, Mordred used the illicit romance to stir up trouble.

Guinevere Loves Mordred?

By the time Thomas Malory wrote Le Morte d'Arthur, *it was well established in the Arthurian legends that Guinevere had a relationship with Lancelot behind Arthur's back. But in Geoffrey of Monmouth's earlier* History of the Kings of Britain, *excerpted here, Lancelot does not appear and Guinevere takes Mordred's side, and bed, against Arthur.*

When summer came, [Arthur] made ready to set out for Rome, and was already beginning to make his way through the mountains when the news was brought to him that his nephew Mordred, in whose care he had left Britain, had placed the crown upon his own head. What is more, the treacherous tyrant was living adulterously and out of wedlock with Queen Guinevere, who had broken the vows of her earlier marriage. About this particular matter . . . Geoffrey of Monmouth prefers to say nothing.

tled knight named Sir Agrivane. As T.H. White told it, together they boldly approached the king and Mordred said, "We have to tell my uncle something and it is right that he should know." Arthur, who had long suspected Mordred of being a gossipmonger and a troublemaker, said he was not so sure he wanted to hear it. But before he could walk away, his nephew blurted out: "We came to tell you what every person in this court has always known. Queen Guinevere is Sir Lancelot's mistress openly!"[48]

The Trap and the Queen's Arrest

Arthur glowered sternly at the men for a long moment. Then he asked them if they were prepared to prove this serious accusation. They replied that they were quite prepared. In fact, Mordred said (according to White), he had a plan to trap the lovers red-handed, after which they would have to be punished for committing the offense of treason against the Crown. "If you would consent, uncle, to go away for the night, we should get together an armed band and capture Lancelot in the queen's room. You would have to be away or he wouldn't go there." After a long pause, Arthur said gravely:

You have our permission. But if I may speak for a moment, Mordred and Agrivane, as a private person, the only hope I now have left is that Lancelot will kill you both and all the witnesses—a feat which, I am proud to say, has never been beyond my Lancelot's power. And I may add this also, as a minister of justice, that if you fail for one moment in

As he leaves Guinevere's apartment, Lancelot confronts several knights.

establishing [the truth of] this monstrous accusation, I shall pursue you both remorselessly, with all the rigor of the laws which you yourselves have set in motion.[49]

Arthur did not purposely leave Camelot to aid Mordred's nefarious plan; but in time the king did have occasion to go on a hunting trip that took him away for the night. It was then that Mordred and Agrivane convinced some other knights to lay in wait with them secretly outside Guinevere's bedchamber. Sure enough, shortly before midnight Sir Lancelot appeared, knocked quietly on the door, and entered with the queen's permission. At this, the concealed knights leapt from their hiding places and raised a loud uproar. They tried to apprehend Lancelot, but he escaped.

When Arthur returned from his hunting trip, he was distressed to find Guinevere in custody and formally accused of treason. He had devoted much of his adult life to establishing and maintaining the rule of law in his land. So he had no choice but to allow the queen to stand trial; thanks to the damning evidence provided by Mordred and his accomplices, she was condemned to be burned at the stake.

This was not to be Guinevere's fate, however. Arthur, as well as many of his closest knights, including Gawain, were counting on Lancelot to arrive in the nick of time and rescue her. That way the law would be satisfied, yet the queen would be spared the pain of death. Accordingly, the valiant Lancelot did not disappoint anyone. As Guinevere stood atop the stake with her hands tied to a pole, he arrived on a magnificent white steed, raised his sword, and plowed into the soldiers standing around her. "And those who stood guard at the stake were slain," wrote Malory,

for none of them could withstand [the onslaught of] Sir Lancelot. . . . Then when Sir Lancelot had done this, and had put them all to flight, he rode straight to Queen Guinevere . . . and had her sit behind him on his horse, and prayed her to be of good cheer. . . . And so he rode away with the queen to Joyous Gard.[50]

The Siege of Joyous Gard

Although, on the one hand, Arthur was overjoyed that his wife had been saved from a gruesome death, on the other, he was stricken with grief for those who had fallen to Lancelot's sword. In addition to the guards, several knights had been slain, among them Gawain's brothers (and Arthur's nephews), Sir Gaheris and Sir Gareth. This turned Gawain, who had been one of Lancelot's truest friends, against him; and thereafter Gawain steadfastly counseled his uncle the king to make war on Lancelot. At first, Arthur could not find it in his heart to attack Lancelot. But Gawain pestered him seemingly night and day until the king finally relented and let the embittered knight have his way.

And so a great host of soldiers marched north from Camelot, carrying with them many weapons and engines of siege warfare. These forces surrounded and laid siege to Joyous Gard. As described by one Arthurian writer:

Its slated turrets, conical in the French fashion, crowded from complicated battlements. . . . There were outside staircases. . . . Real stain-glass windows, high up and out of danger, gleamed. . . . Banner poles, crucifixes, gargoyles, water-spouts, weather-cocks, spires, and belfries crowded the angled roofs—roofs going this way and that, sometimes of red tile, sometimes of mossy stone, sometimes of slate. The place was a town, not a castle.[51]

Joyous Gard was so well defended that the best strategy was to wait until the besieged were hungry enough to come out and fight. But Lancelot refused to fight Arthur, nor would he allow any of his soldiers to do so. When a full fifteen weeks had gone by, the master of the castle climbed atop the battlements and, according to Malory, addressed the king and Gawain this way: "My lords both, hear me well that it is in vain that you labor at this siege, for here you will win nothing but dishonor. Alas, to ride out of this castle and do battle, I'm very loathe to do it."

"What shall we do, then?" asked Sir Gawain. "Is not the king's quarrel with you serious enough to fight over? And it is my own quarrel to fight with you, Lancelot, because of the death of my brothers."[52]

Hearing this, Lancelot reluctantly agreed to do battle. The following morning he rode out of the castle at the head of his troops, and the two armies crashed together. Many men were slain that day, though Arthur, Gawain, and Lancelot survived, each fully expecting to continue the fight the next day and the next, with no end to the carnage in sight.

Lancelot Condemned to Exile

In the meantime, however, far away in the city of Rome, the Pope had heard how some noble Christian knights were laying siege to other noble Christian knights, and he was sorely troubled by the news. His Holiness was also unhappy to hear that the British queen was living in sin with Sir Lancelot. So the Pope sent a messenger to Britain with orders to arrange a truce and conference between the two sides in hopes that peace and Guinevere's return to her rightful husband would be the results. To this meeting, which took place near Camelot, Lancelot brought along the queen, and, according to Malory:

Sir Lancelot spoke such noble words that all the knights and ladies who were present wept to hear him, and the tears fell down King Arthur's cheeks. But the king, to gratify Gawain's revenge for the loss of his brothers, had already promised that Lancelot should be banished, and now . . . he allowed Sir Gawain to declare to Sir Lancelot his doom of exile, that he was forbidden to abide in Britain.[53]

Then Sir Lancelot sighed, and the tears fell down his cheeks. "Alas, most noble Christian realm," he said, "whom I have loved above all other realms, in you have I gotten a great part of my honor, and now I shall depart in this wise!"

Lancelot sadly bids farewell to Guinevere shortly before returning her to Arthur's court.

Then Sir Lancelot bade good-bye to Queen Guinevere in a voice loud enough for the king and all present to hear. "Madame," he said, "now I must depart from you and this noble fellowship forever, and since it is so, I beseech you to pray for me, and speak well of me." And therewith Sir Lancelot kissed the queen, and then he said: "Now let us see anyone in this place that dares to say the queen is not true to my lord Arthur!"[54] With that, he brought the queen to the king, and then Sir Lancelot took his leave. And there was neither king, nor duke or earl, baron or knight, lady or gentlewoman, who did not weep, except Sir Gawain. And thus departed Sir Lancelot from the court of King Arthur forever.

During the months that Guinevere had resided at Joyous Gard after her rescue from the fire, many British and French knights had gathered there to defend her and Lancelot. Now that he was banished, Lancelot went to see these good knights and bid them farewell. But to his surprise, they refused to let him depart alone. "Sir," said one who spoke for them all (in Malory's work),

> if you do not choose to abide in this land, not one of the good knights here will fail you. Since it pleased us to help in your distress and troubles in this realm, it shall equally please us to go into other countries with you, and there to serve with you. Shame on him that will leave you! For we all understand that in this

Sir Gawain began as Lancelot's friend but ended up fighting him.

> realm there will now be no quiet, but always strife now that the fellowship of the Round Table is broken.[55]

True to their word, these loyal knights, who numbered nearly one hundred, followed Lancelot by ship across the English Channel to France.

Gawain Fights Lancelot

Arthur was understandably grief-stricken over Lancelot's banishment, as well as the continued disintegration of the order of the Round Table. Adding to the king's discomfort was Gawain's anger, which had not been quenched by Lancelot's exile. Gawain insisted that he wanted to take an army to France and continue to

Arthur in the Movies

Ever since motion pictures rose to prominence as an art form in the early twentieth century, the Arthurian legends have provided fertile ground from which to draw heroic and romantic screen stories and characters. The earliest films in the genre were silent movies based on German composer Richard Wagner's operas *Tristan and Isolde* and *Parsifal,* in which the main characters are major Arthurian knights. Then came several screen versions of American humorist Mark Twain's witty novel *A Connecticut Yankee in King Arthur's Court,* including a silent film (1921), the first talking version, starring Will Rogers (1931), and a musical version with Bing Crosby (1949). Soon swashbuckling epics depicting Arthur, his court, and his knights proliferated, among them *Knights of the Round Table* (1953), with Robert Taylor as Lancelot and Ava Gardner as Guinevere; *Prince Valiant* (1954), with Robert Wagner as the squire-turned-knight from the famous Arthurian comic strip; and *The Sword of Lancelot* (1963), with Cornel Wilde as Lancelot. In a lighter vein are *The Sword in the Stone* (1963), a Walt Disney cartoon based on part of T. H. White's masterpiece, *The Once and Future King, Camelot* (1967), with Richard Harris as Arthur, the film version of the hit Broadway musical of the same name; and *Monty Python and the Holy Grail* (1975), an outrageous spoof of the Arthurian quests. More recent films in the genre are John Boorman's masterful and brooding *Excalibur* (1981) and an ambitious TV miniseries, *Merlin* (1998).

fight his former friend. Though Arthur was king and could have forbidden it, he was also Gawain's blood relative and felt obliged to allow his nephew to seek redress for the deaths of Sir Gaheris and Sir Gareth.

In the meantime, more pressure came to bear on Arthur from Sir Mordred, who also counseled the king to go to France. With Arthur out of the way and the Round Table severely weakened, Mordred reasoned, he might well be able to get his hands on the throne. Eventually, the well-meaning but unknowing Arthur gave in.

Playing right into the treacherous Mordred's hands, he gave the young man temporary charge of the country, and Guinevere as well, and set off with Sir Gawain for France.

Reaching Bayonne, the British forces laid siege to the city, where Lancelot was then residing. Lancelot sent a young damsel with a message to Arthur asking if there might be a treaty or some other kind of reconciliation between them. And the king's first instinct was to accept this offer and make peace with his old friend.

But, as Malory told it, then the king showed the letter to Gawain, who asked him, "My lord, my uncle, what will you do? Will you turn back now that you have come so far on this journey?"

"Nay," said King Arthur, "you know well, Sir Gawain, that I will do as you, my blood kin, advise me. And yet it seems to me that it is not good to refuse Lancelot's offer."[56] To this, the stubborn Gawain replied that he was not at all interested in Lancelot's offers. Gawain told the messenger to take the following words back to her master:

Say you to Sir Lancelot that it is a waste of labor now to sue my uncle for peace. Tell him it is now too late. And say that I, Sir Gawain, send him word that I promise him by the faith I owe to God and to knighthood that I shall never leave Sir Lancelot alone till he has slain me or I him![57]

At first, Lancelot refused to fight his old friend Gawain. But then Gawain pressed the siege for six months, causing so much misery to French soldiers and commoners alike that Lancelot felt he had no choice but to defend the city. The two men met in single combat in an open space beyond the town's main gate. Gawain insisted that they fight at nine in the morning, for he knew that this would give him an advantage; several years before, a holy man had put a spell on him that increased his strength threefold between the hours of nine and noon.

At precisely nine the opposing knights, in Malory's words, "came together with all their horses' might and each struck the other in the midst of his shield; but the knights were so strong, and their spears so big, that their horses . . . fell to the earth."[58] The two men then fought on foot, swinging their huge swords so hard that deep dents began to mar their shields. For a long while Gawain had the best of it, thanks to his increased, unnatural strength. But then the fight went on past noon, at which time his strength returned to normal, and soon the tide of battle shifted in Lancelot's favor.

Finally, Lancelot gave his opponent a mighty whack on the helmet that sent him reeling to the ground. The victor sighed heavily, then turned and walked away. "Why do you withdraw?" Gawain demanded. "Now turn again, false traitor knight, and slay me!"

Stopping briefly, Lancelot answered, "Sir, I shall never strike a fallen knight."[59] And then he continued on his way and disappeared back into the city.

Arthur was overjoyed that both of his friends had survived the fight. But his joy was soon tempered with alarm and apprehension. A messenger arrived from Britain with ill tidings, namely that in the king's absence Mordred had usurped the throne. Arthur now turned homeward with a heavy heart, hoping that there was still time to save some remnant of the noble fellowship that had been the envy of the world.

Chapter Six

The Passing of Arthur

Arthur had good reason to make haste in returning to his realm, for in his absence, Mordred had been putting into practice a dastardly scheme. While Arthur had been gone for several months, his unscrupulous nephew had forged several letters, making it look as though they had come from the king's scribes in France. According to these false documents, a great battle had taken place in which Sir Lancelot had slain Arthur; moreover, the letters alleged, the surviving knights were in turmoil and pleading for Mordred to lead them.

Pretending to be sad over his uncle's death and concerned for the good of the country, Mordred summoned a parliament, a meeting of the major lords, churchmen, and commoners. He read them the letters and called on them to choose a new king. He also reminded them that he was the one Arthur had left in charge of the realm, which made him the most qualified and logical choice for the succession. The parliament agreed and the archbishop of Canterbury placed the crown on Mordred's head.

Almost immediately after assuming the throne, Mordred sent for Guinevere. He informed her that he intended to marry her and that preparations for the wedding ceremony and feast were already under way. Hearing this, the queen was troubled. Not only did she find Mordred repulsive, she could not conceive of loving or marrying anyone but Arthur or Lancelot. But she realized that Mordred now had the power, and to oppose him openly might mean her doom; so she pretended to be happy about the impending marriage and asked for permission to go to London to buy fabric for her wedding dress. Mordred was completely taken in by her act and agreed.

Once she had reached the ancient British capital, Guinevere acted quickly. She bought up large amounts of food and supplies and gathered together a small group of Arthur's most trusted knights. With these she retired to the fortress of the Tower of London and barricaded it in preparation for a siege. When Mordred learned that the queen had deceived him, according to Malory,

> he went and laid a mighty siege to the Tower of London, and assaulted it with great siege engines, but he

could not prevail. He tried in all ways, by letters and messages, to make Queen Guinevere come out of the Tower, but it availed him nothing; neither for fair words nor foul would the queen trust herself again in the traitor's hands. She answered shortly that she would rather slay herself than marry him.[60]

The Passing of Sir Gawain

Meanwhile, Arthur was in the midst of leading his army across the English Channel. Word of his approach came to Mordred, who trembled at the thought of

The Tower of London, where Guinevere sought refuge from Mordred.

having to face a war hero of Arthur's stature. The usurper reasoned that his best chance to stop his adversary was to destroy Arthur's army as it landed on the beaches and had not yet had time to form ranks. So Mordred led his own forces to the coast at Dover and made ready. He did not have to wait long. "There came King Arthur with a great navy of ships and many galleys," Malory wrote.

> There was launching of great boats and small, and full of noble men of arms, and there was much slaughter of gentle knights, and many a bold baron was laid low on both sides. But King Arthur was so courageous that there were no knights who could keep him from reaching the land, and his own knights fiercely followed him. And so they landed, in spite of Mordred and all his power, and pushed Mordred back, forcing him to flee with all his people.[61]

As Arthur and some of his followers were collecting and burying their dead in the wake of the bloody encounter, they came across a beached boat that at first looked to be empty; but then a moan was heard from the vessel, and on closer inspection they found Sir Gawain inside. For some time he had been suffering mightily from the wounds he had received in his fight with Lancelot. These had reopened during the battle on the beach, and now the noble Gawain lay near death.

Rushing to his nephew's side, Arthur exclaimed that his grief was almost too much to bear. Gawain and Lancelot were the two men in the world he cared about most; and he was losing them both. Gently taking the king's hand, Gawain said:

> My uncle, King Arthur, mark you well that my death day has indeed come, and all this trouble is the result of my own hastiness and willfulness. Had Sir Lancelot been with you as he used to be, this unhappy war would never have begun, and of all this I am the cause. I pray you let me have paper, pen, and ink, that I may write to Sir Lancelot a letter with my own hand.[62]

After some scribes had brought Gawain paper and pen, he began the letter by greeting Lancelot as the "flower of all noble knights that ever I heard of or saw in my days." Then he told Lancelot that he was not to blame for their feud; instead, it had been Sir Gawain himself, who through his own anger and stubbornness had brought about his own death. Then Gawain wrote:

> I beseech you, Lancelot, to return again to this realm and see my tomb, and pray some prayer more or less for my soul. Also, Lancelot, for all the love that has ever been between us, do not tarry, but come over the sea in all the haste that you

can with your noble knights and rescue that noble king who made you a knight, that is my lord and uncle, King Arthur, for he is sorely beset with a false traitor, which is Sir Mordred. This letter was written but two hours and a half before my death, written with my own hand, and so subscribed with part of my heart's blood.[63]

Shortly after sealing the letter, the great and noble Sir Gawain died. Arthur and his whole army stood for a long moment in silence out of a deep-felt love and respect.

On the Field of Camlann

Arthur now pursued Mordred across southern Britain, intent on catching and punishing the usurper. Along the way, the true king stopped in London to collect Guinevere, who was relieved to see him alive, as she, like everyone else, had believed Mordred's lies. Together they journeyed westward to Camelot to find that Mordred and his followers had already fled. Word came that they were on the Plain of Salisbury, where they intended to make their last stand. Arthur was determined that this should indeed be the last time anyone would try to seize the throne and the realm. After all of his remaining loyal knights had joined his ranks, he bade the queen farewell and set out, grim and resolute, for Salisbury and an uncertain destiny.

On a cold, desolate autumn night, the opposing armies camped a few miles apart on the edge of the plain near a place called Camlann. Arthur had trouble falling asleep; but once he did, he had a strange and fantastic dream. "It seemed to him," Malory wrote,

> that he sat on a platform, in a chair, clad in the richest cloth of gold that could be made; and the chair was fastened to a wheel. And the king

Arthur, depicted here, finally confronted Mordred on the Plain of Salisbury.

Shadows in the Mist

In this excerpt from his famous Idylls of the King *(Henry Van Dyke's edition), poet Alfred Tennyson paints stark and somber images of Arthur's final battle at Camlann.*

And there, that day when the great light of heaven
Burn'd at his lowest in the rolling year,
On the waste sand by the waste sea they [the two armies] closed.
Nor ever yet had Arthur fought a fight
Like this last, dim, weird battle of the west.
A deathwhite mist slept over sand and sea:
Whereof the chill, to him who breathed it, drew
Down with his blood, till all his heart was cold
With formless fear; and ev'n on Arthur fell
Confusion, since he saw not whom he fought.
For friend and foe were shadows in the mist,
And friend slew friend not knowing whom he slew....
And ever and anon with host to host
Shocks, and the splintering spear, the hard [chain]mail hewn,
Shield-breakings, and the clash of brands, the crash
Of battleaxes on shatter'd helms, and shrieks
After the Christ, of those who falling down
Look'd up for heaven, and only saw the mist.

thought that under him, far from him, was a hideous deep black water, and therein were all manner of serpents, and worms, and wild beasts, foul and horrible. And suddenly, the king thought, the wheel turned upside down, and he fell among the serpents, and every beast seized him by a limb![64]

Arthur screamed and woke up in a cold sweat. Two knights and some pages rushed into his tent to see if he was all right, and both he and they were relieved to find that he had only been dreaming. The king thanked them for their concern and laid awake a long time, afraid to go back to sleep. But eventually his eyes grew heavy and again he slept; and again he dreamed. This time he thought that Sir Gawain came to him and warned him not to fight Mordred the next morning, for if he did he would be mortally wounded. It would be more prudent, the phantom Gawain advised, to make a truce for a month. That would give Lancelot time to arrive with reinforcements. Having said this, the dream spirit vanished and Arthur awoke a second time.

The king could not be sure that Sir Gawain had really visited him. But it seemed to Arthur that the knight's counsel seemed well-founded, so he sent a messenger to Mordred with an offer for a truce. Because Mordred had been dreading the upcoming battle, he welcomed the proposal and agreed that he and Arthur would meet in an open field between the two armies; each leader could bring fourteen men along as bodyguards. Before walking out to meet Mordred, the king warned his captains to keep a wary eye out for treachery. If they saw an enemy sword drawn, they must attack at once and destroy the usurper and his troops. Mordred gave similar orders to his own officers.

Meeting on the field of Camlann, Arthur and Mordred exchanged greetings guardedly but cordially. Then they began discussing the terms of the truce, including where Mordred would winter his army and the location of their next meeting, where a more lasting peace might be decided. While the two leaders conversed, one of the knights with them suddenly felt a sharp sting on his foot. Looking down he saw a snake, and without thinking he drew his sword to kill it.

At that instant the soldiers in both armies saw the drawn weapon, though at so great a distance that no one could tell whose it was, so all assumed the worst. With a loud and terrible war cry, they rushed forward and within seconds the battle was joined. Some men were impaled on lances, while others hacked off limbs or had their own limbs cut off. There was nothing Arthur could do to stop this lethal collision of knights, and soon the slaughter became so appalling that he knew he was witnessing the end of all he had worked for.

Arthur stabs Mordred as Mordred swings his sword at Arthur's head.

The Returning of Excalibur

By midday the battlefield was strewn with ghastly heaps of dead men. Besides Arthur himself, of his entire army only Sir Lucan and his brother Sir Bedivere were still standing; while across the field, Mordred was the sole survivor of the opposing host. Sir Lucan, who was badly wounded, saw Arthur preparing to go to Mordred and continue the fight, and the knight tried to persuade the king to refrain. "Sir, let him be," said Lucan (in Malory's words),

> for if you survive this unhappy day you shall right well be revenged on him. God of his great goodness has preserved you until now, therefore for God's sake, my lord, leave it as it is. Blessed be God, you have won the field, for here three of us are alive, whereas with Sir Mordred none are alive. And if you stop now, this wicked day of destiny will be over.[65]

But Arthur would not listen to Lucan's counsel. Grasping his spear in both hands, the king ran at Mordred, crying out, "Traitor, now your death day has come!"[66] Seeing Arthur's onslaught, Mordred grimaced and lifted his sword and shield to defend himself. But he was not fast enough, and the king's spear found its way under the shield and plunged straight into the young man's midsection. Mordred's eyes went wide with horror as he felt the weapon slice through his vital organs. He could sense the dreaded pale of death approaching, but as he was determined to remain a villain to his last breath, he suddenly pushed forward, impaling himself further onto the spear. That brought him face-to-face with his enemy, and he swung his sword upward, piercing Arthur's helmet and skull.

Sir Lucan and Sir Bedivere rushed to their fallen king and fortunately found him still living, though mortally wounded. Carefully, they carried him to a small chapel near the seashore. There Sir Lucan, whose own wounds had steadily worsened, died. As Sir Bedivere began to weep for his brother's passing, Arthur told him he had an errand of the utmost urgency for him to perform. Realizing he had not long to live, the king reasoned that he had no further use for the marvelous sword that had been entrusted to him long ago by the Lady of the Lake; and he thought it proper to return it to its rightful owner. "Take you Excalibur, my good sword," Arthur said, his voice thin and weak, "and go with it to yonder shore; and when you get there I charge you to throw my sword into the water, and then come back and tell me what you saw."[67]

Sir Bedivere assured the king he would accomplish this task and carried the sword to the shore. But before throwing it into the water, the knight examined it closely and marveled at the jewels on the pommel and hilt and the fine workmanship. It would be a shame to discard such a magnificent weapon,

After returning Excalibur to the lake, Sir Bedivere watches the mysterious hand carry the weapon downward and out of sight.

he thought, for what possible good could come of it? So Bedivere laid Excalibur under a tree and returned to the ailing Arthur. "What did you see?" the dying man asked (in Malory's version).

"Sir," Bedivere replied, "I saw nothing but waves and winds."

"That is untruly spoken," Arthur said. "Therefore, go quickly again and do as I commanded. Throw the sword in the water!"[68]

Fully intending to do as the king had ordered, Sir Bedivere hurried to the tree and found the sword. But once more he hesitated, thinking it a sin to waste such a splendid artifact. Again the knight returned to Arthur and lied; and again the king saw through the deceit. Finally, on the third try, Bedivere did as he was

In this undated woodcut, the mortally wounded Arthur is borne away to Avalon. It is said he still dwells there, waiting to be recalled.

told and hurled noble Excalibur out over the water. He watched in amazement as a woman's hand suddenly emerged from the waves and caught the weapon in midflight; three times the hand brandished the sword, as if preparing to use it against a foe, and then both hand and sword disappeared into the depths.

Returning again to his sovereign lord, Bedivere carried him down to the water's edge. There they saw a mysterious barge approaching the shore, and on board were three women dressed in black with hoods concealing their faces. "Now put me into the barge,"[69] Arthur commanded Bedivere. Once this had been done, the king saw the ladies' faces and recognized them as queens of small kingdoms bordering his own. Weeping for him, they began to row the barge away from the shore, an action that discomforted Sir Bedivere. Trying to calm him, Arthur called out: "Comfort yourself. I am bound for the isle of Avalon, to heal me of my grievous wound. And if you never hear more of me, pray for my soul!"[70]

The King That Was and Shall Be

After that, the distraught Sir Bedivere wandered aimlessly about the countryside for several days. Finally he came to a monastery in Glastonbury, where the monks claimed that three women had recently brought a dead body; the holy men had buried it in a tomb near their chapel, and they showed the knight the tomb. Assuming the body had been King Arthur's and that this was his final resting place, Bedivere pledged to remain in the monastery and to serve the monks faithfully for the rest of his days.

In the meantime, in faraway France Sir Lancelot had received Gawain's letter urging him to return to Britain with all haste and to aid the king in his struggle

Camelot: A Fleeting Wisp of Glory

In both The Once and Future King, *the famous novel by T.H. White, and the musical* Camelot, *based on that work, Arthur encounters a boy named Tom shortly before the last fateful battle. Tom's enthusiasm for the spirit of the Round Table gives the king hope that the principles of justice he has established will live on. This is an excerpt from the finale of* Camelot.

ARTHUR: From the stories people tell you wish to be a knight? (*A strange light comes into his eyes*) What do you think you know of the knights of the Round Table?

TOM: I know everything, my lord. Might for right! Right for right! Justice for all! A Round Table where all knights would sit. Everything! (*Arthur walks away. Then suddenly he turns to the boy with a trembling inner excitement*)

ARTHUR: Come here, my boy.... Listen to me, Tom of Warwick. You will not fight in the battle, do you hear? ...You will run behind the lines and hide in a tent till it is over. Then you will return to your home in England. Alive. To grow up and grow old. Do you understand?

TOM: Yes, my lord.

ARTHUR: And for as long as you live you will remember what I, the king, tell you; and you will do as I command.

TOM: Yes, my lord.

ARTHUR: Each evening from December to December, before you drift to sleep upon your cot, think back on all the tales you remember of Camelot. Ask every person if he's heard the story; and tell it strong and clear if he has not: that once there was a fleeting wisp of glory called Camelot!

against Mordred. Responding to this call, Lancelot wasted no time in gathering together a band of trusted knights and crossing the Channel to Dover. There he received the distressing news of the slaughter at Camlann, including the wounding, disappearance, and presumed death of the king. According to Malory, Lancelot said, "Alas! These are the heaviest tidings that have ever come to me."[71]

Remembering Gawain's last request—that Lancelot should visit his tomb—Lancelot sought it out and found it near Dover Castle. He knelt and wept and prayed heartily for Gawain's soul. Then

Lancelot searched for Guinevere and found her in a nunnery lying seven days' ride from the coast. Crushed by Arthur's reported death and the collapse of the Round Table, she had committed herself to live out the rest of her years in service to God. Seeing Lancelot again, she kept him at arm's length and fought back the tears when she said: "Lancelot, I beseech you heartily, for all the love that there was between us, that you never look at me again. Pray for me unto our Lord God that I may make amends for my sins."[72]

Deeply saddened, Lancelot departed from the nunnery, and, holding true to the

Was Glastonbury the Fabled Avalon?

Where was the Isle of Avalon, Arthur's mysterious resting place? Some modern scholars suggest that Glastonbury, an ancient monastery atop a steep hill in southern England, may be that fabled place. Some evidence shows that the hill was surrounded by lake water in early medieval times, making it an island at the time. Also, in Malory's Le Morte d'Arthur *and other late medieval works, Glastonbury is the spot where the monks place Arthur's body in a tomb. These writers based this plot twist on the supposed discovery of Arthur's bones by Glastonbury monks in the year 1191. A twelfth-century writer named Gerald of Wales (quoted from Richard White's* King Arthur in Legend and History) *recorded:*

In our own lifetime, Arthur's body was discovered at Glastonbury....The body was hidden deep in the earth ... between two stone pyramids which had been set up long ago in the churchyard there. They [the monks] carried it into the church with every mark of honor and buried it there decently in a marble tomb....Beneath it—and not on top as would be the custom nowadays—there was a stone slab, with a leaden cross attached to its underside. I have seen this cross myself and I have traced the lettering....The inscription read as follows: HERE IN THE ISLE OF AVALON LIES BURIED THE RENOWNED KING ARTHUR.

request of the woman he loved, he never again gazed on her while she was living. He traveled to Glastonbury, where he found Sir Bedivere still in service to the monks, and Sir Bors, too. Lancelot joined them there, becoming a monk himself and serving humbly for seven long years. Then one day word came that Guinevere had died, and he and the other former knights requested that her body be brought to Glastonbury and interred there in Arthur's tomb. After this, as Malory put it,

The supposed site of Arthur's tomb in Glastonbury.

Sir Lancelot fell ill, eating and drinking little, and gradually pining away, for there was nothing anyone could do to comfort him. Evermore, day and night he prayed . . . and often he was found lying on the tomb of King Arthur and Queen Guinevere. At last he grew so weak that he could no longer rise from bed, and then he sent for the good Bishop . . . and begged that he might receive the last sacred rights of religion. . . . That night, while all lay asleep, the good Bishop had a beautiful dream. He thought he saw Sir Lancelot surrounded with a great throng of angels, and they carried him up to heaven. . . . [The next morning] when Bors and the other knights came to Sir Lancelot's bed, they found him stark dead, and there was a smile on his face.[73]

One thing Lancelot had wondered about during his sad and lonely last days was whether Arthur was really dead. Now Sir Bors and the others wondered the same thing. No one could be sure that the bones that lay in the king's tomb were really those of Arthur Pendragon; and already there had been reports of people claiming to have seen the former king walking alone along the misty moors on moonlit nights.

And so it was that people in those parts came to believe in their hearts that Arthur was not dead at all, but that he lived on in the mystical Avalon or some other remote place. He would return someday, they said, when Britain needed him most, and once more establish a brotherhood and realm of goodness and justice. In that way, the man whom they saw as the greatest hero of their time would be transformed into a hero for the ages. Inspired by this vision, an unknown person at some unknown date inscribed the following words on the tomb at Glastonbury: "Here lies Arthur, the King that was, and the King that shall be."[74]

NOTES

Introduction: Arthur's Place in Western Culture

1. Christopher Snyder, *The World of King Arthur.* London: Thames and Hudson, 2000, p. 8.
2. Richard Barber, ed., *The Arthurian Legends: An Illustrated Anthology.* New York: Peter Bedrick Books, 1979, p. 2.
3. Graham Phillips and Martin Keatman, *King Arthur: The True Story.* London: Century Random House, 1992, p. 3.
4. Snyder, *World of King Arthur,* p. 177.
5. From the finale of *Camelot* (Alan Jay Lerner, *Camelot: A New Musical.* New York: Random House, 1961, p. 114), the Broadway musical based on T.H. White's novel about Arthur, *The Once and Future King.* The full line is: "Don't let it be forgot that once there was a spot, for one brief shining moment, that was known as Camelot."

Chapter 1: Arthur in History, Legend, and Literature

6. Gildas, *On the Ruin of Britain,* in Richard White, ed., *King Arthur in Legend and History.* London: Routledge, 1990, p. 3.
7. Gildas, *On the Ruin of Britain,* in White, *King Arthur,* p. 14.

8. *Welsh Annals,* in Barber, *Arthurian Legends,* p. 7.
9. *History of the Britons,* in Snyder, *World of King Arthur,* p. 77.
10. Leslie Alcock, *Arthur's Britain: History and Archaeology, A.D. 367–634.* New York: Penguin, 1989, pp. 348–49.
11. Quoted in White, *King Arthur,* p. 13.
12. Geoffrey of Monmouth, *The History of the Kings of Britain,* trans. Lewis Thorpe. Baltimore: Penguin, 1966, pp. 217–18.
13. Chrétien de Troyes, *Lancelot, or the Knight of the Cart,* in White, *King Arthur,* p. 157.
14. Barber, *Arthurian Legends,* p. 138.

Chapter 2: The Coming of Arthur

15. T.H. White, *The Once and Future King.* New York: Berkley, 1966, p. 29.
16. Thomas Malory, *Le Morte d'Arthur,* in Sidney Lanier, ed., *King Arthur and His Knights of the Round Table.* New York: Atheneum, 1989, p. 4. Note: To make Malory's old English somewhat more understandable for a modern audience, occasional minor changes in vocabulary and word usage have been made in this and other excerpts used in this book.
17. Malory, *Le Morte d'Arthur,* in Lanier, *Arthur,* p. 4.
18. Malory, *Le Morte d'Arthur,* in Lanier, *Arthur,* p. 5.

19. Malory, *Le Morte d'Arthur*, in Lanier, *Arthur*, pp. 5–6.
20. Malory, *Le Morte d'Arthur*, in Lanier, *Arthur*, p. 7.
21. Malory, *Le Morte d'Arthur*, in Lanier, *Arthur*, p. 9.
22. Malory, *Le Morte d'Arthur*, in Lanier, *Arthur*, p. 9.
23. Malory, *Le Morte d'Arthur*, in Lanier, *Arthur*, p. 11.
24. Malory, *Le Morte d'Arthur*, in Lanier, *Arthur*, p. 12.

Chapter 3: The Order of the Round Table

25. Geoffrey of Monmouth, *History of the Kings of Britain*, p. 215.
26. Geoffrey of Monmouth, *History of the Kings of Britain*, p. 216.
27. Malory, *Le Morte d'Arthur*, in Lanier, *Arthur*, pp. 16–17.
28. Malory, *Le Morte d'Arthur*, in Lanier, *Arthur*, p. 17.
29. Malory, *Le Morte d'Arthur*, in Lanier, *Arthur*, p. 17.
30. Malory, *Le Morte d'Arthur*, in Lanier, *Arthur*, p. 17.
31. Wace, *Roman de Brut* (ca. 1155), in White, *King Arthur*, p. 46.
32. Geoffrey of Monmouth, *History of the Kings of Britain*, p. 222.
33. Thomas Malory, *Le Morte d'Arthur*, in Mary Macleod, *The Book of King Arthur and His Noble Knights*. Philadelphia: J.B. Lippincott, 1949, pp: 33–34.
34. Malory, *Le Morte d'Arthur*, in Macleod, *Book of King Arthur*, p. 35.
35. Malory, *Le Morte d'Arthur*, in Macleod, *Book of King Arthur*, p. 36.
36. Malory, *Le Morte d'Arthur*, in Macleod, *Book of King Arthur*, p. 40.
37. Malory, *Le Morte d'Arthur*, in Macleod, *Book of King Arthur*, pp. 40–41.

Chapter 4: The Coming of Lancelot

38. White, *Once and Future King*, p. 329.
39. White, *Once and Future King*, pp. 329–30.
40. Malory, *Le Morte d'Arthur*, in Lanier, *Arthur*, pp. 21–22.
41. Chrétien de Troyes, *Lancelot*, in White, *King Arthur*, p. 157.
42. Chrétien de Troyes, *Lancelot*, in White, *King Arthur*, p. 157.
43. Lerner, *Camelot*, pp. 69–70.
44. P.M. Matarasso, trans., *The Quest of the Holy Grail*. New York: Penguin Books, 1969, pp. 43–44.
45. Malory, *Le Morte d'Arthur*, in Macleod, *Book of King Arthur*, pp. 291–92.
46. Malory, *Le Morte d'Arthur*, in Macleod, *Book of King Arthur*, p. 293.

Chapter 5: The Treachery of Mordred

47. Malory, *Le Morte d'Arthur*, in Macleod, *Book of King Arthur*, p. 302.
48. White, *Once and Future King*, p. 556.
49. White, *Once and Future King*, pp. 559–60.
50. Malory, *Le Morte d'Arthur*, in Lanier, *Arthur*, pp. 243–44.
51. White, *Once and Future King*, p. 588.

52. Malory, *Le Morte d'Arthur,* in Lanier, *Arthur,* pp. 246–48.
53. Malory, *Le Morte d'Arthur,* in Macleod, *Book of King Arthur,* p. 304.
54. Malory, *Le Morte d'Arthur,* in Macleod, *Book of King Arthur,* pp. 304–5.
55. Malory, *Le Morte d'Arthur,* in Macleod, *Book of King Arthur,* p 306.
56. Malory, *Le Morte d'Arthur,* in Macleod, *Book of King Arthur,* p. 308.
57. Malory, *Le Morte d'Arthur,* in Macleod, *Book of King Arthur,* p. 309.
58. Malory, *Le Morte d'Arthur,* in Lanier, *Arthur,* p. 254.
59. Malory, *Le Morte d'Arthur,* in Lanier, *Arthur,* p. 255.

Chapter 6: The Passing of Arthur

60. Malory, *Le Morte d'Arthur,* in Macleod, *Book of King Arthur,* p. 314.
61. Malory, *Le Morte d'Arthur,* in Lanier, *Arthur,* p. 261.
62. Malory, *Le Morte d'Arthur,* in Macleod, *Book of King Arthur,* p. 315.
63. Malory, *Le Morte d'Arthur,* in Lanier, *Arthur,* pp. 262–63.
64. Malory, *Le Morte d'Arthur,* in Macleod, *Book of King Arthur,* p. 316.
65. Malory, *Le Morte d'Arthur,* in Lanier, *Arthur,* p. 266.
66. Malory, *Le Morte d'Arthur,* in Lanier, *Arthur,* p. 266.
67. Malory, *Le Morte d'Arthur,* in Macleod, *Book of King Arthur,* p. 319.
68. Malory, *Le Morte d'Arthur,* in Macleod, *Book of King Arthur,* p. 319.
69. Malory, *Le Morte d'Arthur,* in Macleod, *Book of King Arthur,* p. 320.
70. Malory, *Le Morte d'Arthur,* in Lanier, *Arthur,* pp. 270–71.
71. Malory, *Le Morte d'Arthur,* in Lanier, *Arthur,* p. 274.
72. Malory, *Le Morte d'Arthur,* in Lanier, *Arthur,* p. 275.
73. Malory, *Le Morte d'Arthur,* in Macleod, *Book of King Arthur,* pp. 323–24.
74. Malory, *Le Morte d'Arthur,* in Macleod, *Book of King Arthur,* p. 321.

FOR FURTHER READING

Catherine M. Andronik, *Quest for a King: Searching for the Real King Arthur.* New York: Atheneum, 1989. Young readers will be fascinated by this exploration into the possibility that Arthur was a real figure who lived in early medieval England.

Rosalind Kerven, *DK Classics: King Arthur.* London: Dorling Kindersley, 1998. A beautifully illustrated introduction to the Arthurian characters and legends, aimed at young readers. Highly recommended.

Anne McCaffrey, *Black Horses of the King.* San Diego: Harcourt Brace, 1996. In this well-written, fast-paced modern Arthurian story, a young Celtic boy helps King Arthur obtain horses to use in his war against the Saxons.

Neil Philip, *The Illustrated Book of Myths: Tales and Legends of the World.* New York: Dorling Kindersley, 1995. An excellent introduction to world mythology for young people, enlivened with many stunning photos and drawings. Includes brief synopses of several Arthurian stories.

Barbara L. Picard, *Stories of King Arthur and His Knights.* New York: Oxford University Press, 1955. Picard, one of the twentieth century's leading interpreters of old literary classics for young people, does a fine job of retelling some of the old romantic tales of Arthurian England.

Mark Twain, *A Connecticut Yankee in King Arthur's Court.* New York: Bantam, 1989. Twain's witty, engaging story about a modern man who is accidentally transported back to Arthurian England remains first-class entertainment for all. Highly recommended.

Evelyn Wolfson, *Arthurian Mythology.* Berkeley Heights, NJ: Enslow, 2002. A brief but informative overview of some of the main Arthurian legends, supplemented by snippets of scholarly commentary.

Major Works Consulted

Leslie Alcock, *Arthur's Britain: History and Archaeology, A.D. 367–634.* New York: Penguin, 1989. Alcock, of the University of Glasgow, led the archaeological excavation of Cadbury Castle, one of the major supposed Arthurian sites in Britain. In this very readable volume, he explores the main Arthurian evidence, attempting to separate myth from historical fact. Highly recommended for those interested in Arthurian lore.

Richard Barber, ed., *The Arthurian Legends: An Illustrated Anthology.* New York: Peter Bedrick Books, 1979. An excellent collection of primary Arthurian sources, enhanced by excellent background information and commentary.

Thomas Bulfinch, *Bulfinch's Mythology.* New York: Dell, 1959. This is one of several versions of this well-known and useful work, which is itself a modern compilation of two of Bulfinch's original books—*The Age of Fable* (1855), a retelling of the Greek and Roman myths, and *The Age of Chivalry* (1858), an account of the Arthurian legends.

David Day, *The Search for King Arthur.* New York: Facts On File, 1995. One of the better modern volumes that sifts through the shadowy historical evidence for early medieval Britain in an attempt to find the real King Arthur (if in fact such a person did exist).

Geoffrey of Monmouth, *The History of the Kings of Britain.* Trans. Lewis Thorpe. Baltimore: Penguin, 1966. The descriptions of King Arthur in this history of Britain, composed circa 1136, inspired Thomas Malory and other later writers to write about the legendary British hero.

Norma L. Goodrich, *King Arthur.* New York: Franklin Watts, 1989. Goodrich, one of the more distinguished modern mythology experts, delivers a highly readable exploration of the literary versus real Arthur.

Sidney Lanier, ed. *King Arthur and His Knights of the Round Table.* New York: Atheneum, 1950. This attractive, readable volume remains the most widely popular abridged version of Thomas Malory's *Le Morte d'Arthur,* retaining large portions of the original.

Alan Jay Lerner, *Camelot: A New Musical.* New York: Random House, 1961. The book and lyrics of the now-classic musical play version of T.H. White's equally classic novel, *The Once and Future King*.

Proinsias Mac Cana, *Celtic Mythology*. New York: Peter Bedrick Books, 1985. A well-organized and informative description of Celtic folklore, including some of the tales of Arthur and the other traditional heroes of yore.

Sir Thomas Malory, *Le Morte d' Arthur*. Ed. John Matthews. London: Sterling Publications, 2000. The latest complete edition of Malory's classic telling of the Arthurian legends.

———, *Works*. Ed. Eugene Vinaver. Rev. P.J.C. Field. 3 vols. Oxford: Clarendon Press, 1990. The most widely used complete version of *Le Morte d' Arthur* during the twentieth century.

P.M. Matarasso, trans., *The Quest of the Holy Grail*. New York: Penguin Books, 1969. Written in the thirteenth century, this anonymous work is one of the most important medieval literary sources telling the story of the search for the Grail.

Christopher Snyder, *The World of King Arthur*. London: Thames and Hudson, 2000. A well-written and exquisitely illustrated overview of Arthurian history, lore, literature, and more. Highly recommended.

John Steinbeck, *The Acts of King Arthur and His Noble Knights*. Ed. Chase Horton. New York: Ballantine, 1976. The great modern novelist tries his hand at updating Thomas Malory's version of the Arthurian legends.

Alfred, Lord Tennyson, *Idylls of the King*. Ed. Henry Van Dyke. New York: American Book, 1904. This poem in ten books is one of the more famous and popular of the modern literary adaptations of the Arthurian legends.

Richard White, ed., *King Arthur in Legend and History*. London: Routledge, 1990. A large and extremely useful compendium of primary Arthurian documents, including excerpts or full texts of various historical as well as literary works concerning Arthur, his knights, Camelot, and so forth.

T.H. White, *The Once and Future King*. New York: Berkley, 1966. Terence Hanbury White wrote his *Sword in the Stone*, about how Arthur became king, in 1938. Twenty years later, he incorporated the text into a larger book covering the complete Arthurian story—*The Once and Future King*. This modern classic, which closely follows the story line of Thomas Malory's version, is recommended for readers of all ages (although it will be challenging for those under twelve).

Additional Works Consulted

Geoffrey Ashe, *Camelot and the Vision of Albion*. New York: St. Martin's Press, 1971.

———, *The Discovery of King Arthur*. New York: Henry Holt, 1985.

———, *King Arthur's Avalon*. New York: Barnes and Noble, 1992.

———, *The Quest for Arthur's Britain*. London: Paladin, 1971.

Michael Ashley, ed., *The Pendragon Chronicles: Heroic Fantasy from the Time of King Arthur*. New York: Wing Books, 1993.

Richard Barber, *King Arthur: Hero and Legend*. New York: Dorset Press, 1990.

Marion Z. Bradley, *The Mists of Avalon*. New York: Del Rey/Ballantine, 2000.

Richard Cavendish, *King Arthur and the Grail*. London: Weidenfeld and Nicolson, 1978.

Nora K. Chadwick and Barry Cunliffe, *The Celts*. New York: Penguin, 1998.

Peter B. Ellis, *The Celtic Empire: The First Millennium of Celtic History, c. 1000 B.C.–51 A.D.* Durham: Carolina Academic Press, 1990.

Patrick K. Ford, ed. and trans., *The Mabinogi and Other Medieval Welsh Tales*. Los Angeles: University of California Press, 1977.

Norma L. Goodrich, *Merlin*. New York: Franklin Watts, 1987.

Miranda J. Green, *Celtic Myths*. Austin: University of Texas Press, 1993.

A.O.H. Jarman and Gwilym Rees, eds., *A Guide to Welsh Literature*. Swansea: Christopher Davies, 1976.

Elizabeth Jenkins, *The Mystery of King Arthur*. New York: Dorset Press, 1990.

Mary Macleod, *The Book of King Arthur and His Noble Knights*. Philadelphia: J. B. Lippincott, 1949.

Eugene Mason, trans., *Arthurian Chronicles*. London: Dent, 1912.

D.D.R. Owen, trans., *Chrétien de Troyes: Arthurian Romances*. London: J.M. Dent, 1987.

Graham Phillips and Martin Keatman, *King Arthur: The True Story*. London: Century Random House, 1992.

Howard Pyle, *The Story of King Arthur and His Knights*. New York: Signet, 1986.

T.C. Rumble, ed., *The Breton Lays in Middle English*. Detroit: Wayne State University Press, 1975.

Brian Stone, trans., *King Arthur's Death*. New York: Penguin, 1988.

———, trans., *Sir Gawain and the Green Knight*. New York: Penguin, 1979.

INDEX

PICTURE CREDITS

ABOUT THE AUTHOR

Historian and award-winning writer Don Nardo has published numerous biographies of important historical figures, including Julius Caesar, Cleopatra, Thomas Jefferson, Charles Darwin, H.G. Wells, and Adolf Hitler. He has also turned out several studies and retellings of classic myths and legends, among them *Heroes, Monsters, Greek Myths* (for basic readers), *Roman Myths* (for basic readers), and the massive *Greenhaven Encyclopedia of Greek and Roman Mythology*. Along with his wife, Christine, Mr. Nardo resides in Massachusetts.